CHOKIO MEMORIES

Norma Jipson Knight

CHOKIO MEMORIES

Norma Knight

Copyright © 2010 by Norma Knight.

Library of Congress Control Number:		2010900613
ISBN:	Hardcover	978-1-4500-2970-4
	Softcover	978-1-4500-2969-8
	Ebook	978-1-4500-2971-1

All rights reserved. No part of this book may be reproduced or transmitted in any form or by any means, electronic or mechanical, including photocopying, recording, or by any information storage and retrieval system, without permission in writing from the copyright owner.

This book was printed in the United States of America.

To order additional copies of this book, contact:
Xlibris Corporation
1-888-795-4274
www.Xlibris.com
Orders@Xlibris.com
75041

Contents

Preface		9
Chapter One	We Arrive	11
Chapter Two	Everybody Works	15
Chapter Three	Other Duties	24
Chapter Four	Our Town	27
Chapter Five	Early Friends and Neighbors	31
Chapter Six	Relatives, Visiting and Otherwise	37
Chapter Seven	Church Friends and Activities	48
Chapter Eight	Extraneous Pursuits	54
Chapter Nine	Sports	61
Chapter Ten	Hobbies and Interests	67
Chapter Eleven	School Days	71
Chapter Twelve	Minnesota Winters	78
Chapter Thirteen	War	80
Chapter Fourteen	A Town Interlude	85
Chapter Fifteen	Our New Farm	89
Epilogue		103
Acknowledgements		105

LaVonne   Norma

DEDICATION

To Kay

Preface

I never intended to write a book, but now I have. This came about as the result of a phone call I received from my eldest daughter, Kay Carlson, requesting me to write something about my life as I was growing up, including the town and the people of that place and period. This book is the culmination of that effort. It has been a pleasant experience actually to write the story, as it has brought back so many memories that had long ago been put to rest. It has also prompted phone calls and emails to and from friends from long ago, which is always a pleasant enjoyable thing.

Now that my entire birth family is gone, I frequently wish I had asked more about some event or circumstance in our lives, especially the whys. There are always things that a child does not perceive or remember or was deliberately shielded from. If this effort prompts others to ask those questions about their own family history and experiences, it will have served a useful purpose.

Every family undoubtedly has some happenings that the elders are reluctant to talk about with their offspring. In our family, my mother had a brother who was never mentioned. I found out that he existed when we were notified of his death in 1944. It was while we were living in the apartment over the hardware store in Chokio. Mother did go to Iowa for the funeral, but when she returned no more was said about him except that he had a wife and children. Even in their last years my parents wouldn't discuss this topic, my father saying only that he was something of a black sheep. Someone once told my sister, LaVonne, that he had gone AWOL during the First World War. It seems complete ostracism from the family is a rather stiff sentence for something like that. Surely one would forgive eventfully, especially considering the fact that there were several members of the Friends religion in my mother's family. Perhaps war was abhorrent to him. Conscientious Objector status was not permitted unless you were an actual member of a church whose by-laws specifically stated that policy. This story still remains unexplained as far as I am concerned.

Our town Chokio (pronounced sha-KI-o) is a Sioux Indian word that means half way. It is located half way between St. Cloud, MN and Fort Wadsworth, which was just west of Sisseton, SD. Supplies for Fort Wadsworth came through the Chokio site or at least very near to Chokio on what was called the Wadsworth Trail. A small trading post was built there as a resting place. The trail was 165 miles long and took 8 to 10 days to travel at that time, around the end of the Civil War. One has to wonder what trials and tribulations occurred while trying to keep supplies flowing to the fort. Winter storms and summer heat combined with the mosquitoes would have made many trips challenging to say the least. Today, Minnesota State Highway 28 follows close to this route, and is a pleasant drive.

The first of our relatives to live in this area were Will and Lil Laughead, and their daughter, Gladys. They moved to Chokio in 1903 from Plover, Iowa, but had originally lived in southern Wisconsin, around Albany and Attica in Green County. My great grandfather, Norman Jipson, who was a brother-in-law to Will Laughead, bought a farm a short distance south of Chokio as an investment. When he passed away during the depression this farm went to his son, Harry Jipson, Sr. and resulted in that family moving from Iowa to Chokio in 1935. We joined these branches of the family in 1936, and so began our Chokio story.

Chapter One

We Arrive

My parents were both born and raised in Northwest Iowa. My father, M. Duane Jipson, was born August 24th, 1910 and my mother, Edith Hill, was born February 13th, 1905. My father's family came to North America in the 1630's from England and owned property in Boston. Mother had an ancestor who fought in the Revolutionary War with the British forces and stayed after the war ended. Mother used to say that that war was not completely settled, at least in our family. My parents were married on August 24th, 1929 on my father's 19th birthday. Two months later the stock market crashed, and we all know what followed.

Chokio is a small town located in west central Minnesota. Most people have never heard of it, but to me and to those people who grew up and lived there, it was special. My father first went there in January of 1936 to attend the funeral of a relative. While there he decided he liked the area and land was less expensive than in Iowa, where we were living, so he purchased a 160 acre farm from Uncle Will Laughead for $40.00 per acre. And we became Minnesotans.

Morris was our county seat (Stevens County) and was the "big town" in our area with around 3000 people. They had things like doctors, dentists, & lawyers. I was with my father one day in a store in Morris when two Roman Catholic sisters walked in. I said, "Look, Daddy, witches!" Just one of my father's more embarrassing moments. I had never seen a nun before, having always lived near very small towns.

My parents wedding photo Edith & Duane Jipson

We moved to Chokio in December of 1936 when I was 5 & my sister, LaVonne, was 6. Incredibly, I cannot remember the drive up, which was about 200 miles. The farm we were moving to had previously been rented to Dewitt Bennett. The Bennett's were retiring and had built a new house in Chokio. Since they had thus vacated the farm house, we were allowed to move in before the March 1st date that was customary. It seems incredible that my parents would move before the holidays, leaving all close relatives behind, and, in addition, LaVonne was ill with pneumonia. But the house in Iowa was impossible to heat, and they must have decided that it was better to risk the move than stay longer there. Both my sister & I suffered from chill blains as a result of living in that cold Iowa house, even though my father would get up in the night to tend to the fire. I remember having intermittent leg pains until I was in my teens.

At first, we moved in with Isabel Jipson, an aunt of my father's, as our new home had been unheated for a period of time and wouldn't be ready for occupancy until stoves could be set up & operational long enough to make it livable. There would have been a wood burning stove in the kitchen and an oil burning stove in the living room. There was a floor opening in our bedroom upstairs, to let heat from the first floor rise and add a little warmth to our bedroom.

This radiator, as it was called, also served as a listening devise when we had been sent to bed just as our favorite radio program was about to begin. Fibber McGee & Molly was our favorite and came on at 8 pm on Tuesdays. On Tuesdays, LaVonne and I would be bent over the radiator listening as quietly as possible. This would not be a good time to laugh out loud.

Returning to the time of our arrival, a doctor was summoned for LaVonne, and he said that she should not be moved until she was better. I have a letter regarding the stay and stating that Lillian, aged 11, washed all the dishes and Norma wiped. Isabel's household consisted of her sons, Ralph & Fayette, and daughters, Myrta & Lillian, in addition to herself. Her husband, Harry Sr. & son, Harry Jr. aged fourteen, had both died earlier that year, also from pneumonia. Add to that four members of our family and you see I'm talking about a lot of dishes. This at a time when all things were made from scratch! This family had had a very bad year, and it was truly charitable of them to welcome us after just losing two family members also to pneumonia.

Eventually Ralph & Fayette assumed the running of this farm, and Isabel built a home in Chokio where she was employed for many years by Nelson's store. Years later she married Jim Graham, who had also lost his wife. Fayette stayed in the Chokio area, but Ralph eventually bought a farm near Dumont, MN. Myrta married Russell Diehl and they resided in the Donnelly, MN area. Lillian married Leo Benham and they stayed in the Chokio area until they retired when they moved to Morris.

Our new farm home had 8 rooms plus two unheated porches. The room arrangement was unimaginative, but still a great improvement over our former house in Iowa. LaVonne & I shared one bedroom and had another room, which could only be entered from our bedroom, as a play room. Quite a luxury for 2 little girls!

Once the stoves had worked their magic, this house was much warmer and quite comfortable, although we always dressed warmly in the winter. We wore dresses, petticoats, and ugly long brown stockings over long underwear. Girls did not wear slacks in those days. Those ugly socks were held in place by harness-like garters that went over our shoulders and hung down on both sides. It took a bit of care to get the stockings on neatly over the long underwear. My father would help one of us while Mother helped the other girl.

All girls hated those long brown stockings, and the lucky ones had mothers who let them switch to anklets in early spring. I was the last one wearing them in my class. Well, actually Audrey Wensman wore them a long time too, but she lived in town and went home at noon. Her mother let her wear anklets in the afternoon, when presumably it had warmed up.

For outdoor activities in those long, cold Minnesota winters, we wore a snow suit, which consisted of woolen leggings & jacket. Some type of head gear would also be worn, of course. With overshoes for our feet and mittens for our hands, we were all bundled up for outdoor play.

A back porch led to the kitchen and contained a hand pump that drew water from the cistern below. Rain water from the cistern was carried by pails to the reservoir on the cook stove. Using the stove kept the reservoir water a comfortable temperature for hand washing. There were no built in cupboards, the sink was mounted on a wall, and a table sat in the middle of the room. There was no running water, but a drain carried the water away to a creek that ran through our farm. All soaps were biodegradable at this time.

We kept our jackets, overshoes and other outerwear in this porch during mild weather, but cold weather found them brought into the kitchen and kept in one corner on hooks. This did not improve the décor, but the house completely lacked closets.

The cistern water was not used for drinking, as it was unfiltered run-off from the roof. We carried pails full of water to the house from a well in the yard for drinking. The pail sat next to the sink and held a dipper. You drank from the dipper and anything you didn't drink was put back into the pail. Guests used the same procedure. We had no more illnesses than today, as exposure to microbes helps to maintain immunity. Wells had to be placed away from drainage areas and barn yards. Typhoid could be contracted from improperly placed or maintained wells, which might allow surface water to seep in.

The well also served as our refrigerator during warm weather. We had a bucket tied on the end of a rope that was lowered into the well and held things like milk, butter, etc. Most leftovers from dinner, which was served at noon, were eaten at the evening meal the same day, thus not requiring refrigeration. The evening meal was called supper.

The toilet facilities consisted of an outhouse supplied with last year's Montgomery Ward catalog. During fruit canning season, we had the luxury of tissue paper as it was used to wrap the fruit purchased by the crate.

In addition to the house, the building site consisted of an almost new barn, a hog house, a granary, a chicken house and the aforementioned outhouse. My father decided that we should have a garage and drew up some plans. With further pondering, he thought that if he turned the building 90 degrees and extended it a few feet, it could hold two vehicles and thus accommodate the tractor, too. Before starting on the construction, he determined that if he added some more—well, it finally ended up being a machine shed large enough to hold the combine & other farm equipment. He did eventually build a garage, but that was a few years later.

Chapter Two

Everybody Works

Mother washed clothes in a wringer style Maytag washer in the basement. The stairs to the basement were entered through a trap door in the pantry, off the kitchen and below the stairs to the 2nd floor. All of our canned goods, potatoes and other root vegetables were stored in the basement, too. It was a dark and not very interesting place. I remember one day being sent to the basement to get something, when I spotted a green object that looked pretty. I picked it up and it was a live lizard. I was horrified and let out a scream. My parents thought the lizard must have come in through the floor drain all the way from the creek.

To actually wash the clothes my mother had to pump the water from the cistern and fill a boiler on the cook stove in the kitchen. This would be heated to boiling and then carried down to the basement to fill the washing machine. Clothes were rinsed in cold water, which also had to be carried to the basement from the cistern. People without floor drains had to carry the wash water out again. And they needed to carry it some distance away from the house because it would draw flies. Flies were a common problem on farms due to the presence of livestock. My father thought that not putting in a floor drain was foolish. It required some hard work, a relatively small monetary outlay, but saved the wife a lot of time and work.

We always washed on Monday and ironed on Tuesday. Clothes to be ironed (and everything had to be ironed) would be sprinkled and rolled up tight, then left overnight. Irons were just that, iron. We had three bases, which were heated on the kitchen stove, and a detachable handle. When the one you were using became too cool, you just switched to another base. We covered the ones that were being heated with a large cast iron skillet to keep the heat in. You always wiped the iron across a piece of clean paper before touching it to the clothing, or you might leave a dark streak on the garment.

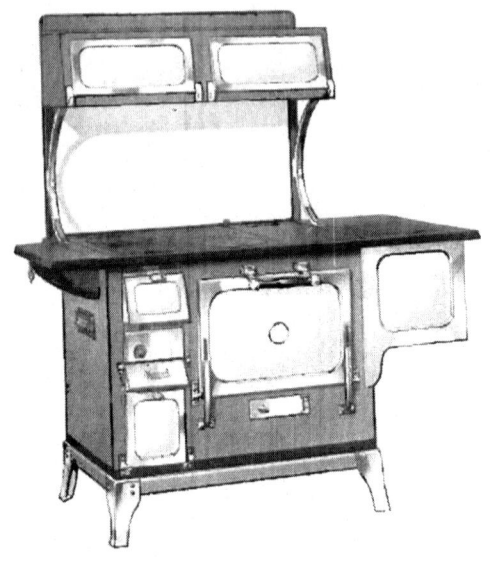

Monarch Range with High Closet and Water Reservoir

The work load, for both adults, was really something and seemed to be without end. My father was willing to help Mother when he was around the house or yard, but I remember some women who got little or no help from their spouses. I still feel sorry for some of them when I think about it. Also, I just don't believe it when I hear politicians say that people are working harder then ever today. Where do they come from? Not from my era.

Farm wives were the original working women as most had more to do than just tend to the home and family. Care of the chickens usually fell to the wife. This included the carrying of feed and water, gathering eggs, cleaning out nests, treating any illnesses, and so forth. After the eggs were gathered, they were washed and packed for sale. Plus, the cream separator had to be washed and reassembled daily. We never had hired help in the house as some people did; my mother did it all.

Harvest time was especially hard work for everyone. Those who owned threshing machines formed what were called "rings." All farmers in a given ring were obligated to assist with the harvest at every other farm that was in the ring. Each farmer brought a team of horses and a hay rack, and at day's end, drove the team and hay rack home again. Grain from the threshing machine was elevated into wagons and then taken to a storage site. The straw was blown out a blower and left in a large stack. Straw from the stack could be used as bedding for livestock. The threshing machine was moved to each farm and stayed until their grain was all harvested, then moved to the next farm.

The small grain, such as oats, wheat, barley, rye and flax, would have been previously cut and tied into bundles, by a machine called a binder and then put into shocks by hand. It took eight bundles to construct one shock. This was hot, dry August weather, and there is no shade in grain fields. I know of one hired man who died from heat stroke while shocking grain, but that was in Iowa.

The only year I actually remember the thresher being at our farm, LaVonne & I were paid to do dishes. We were so slow that Mother would change the water from time to time, and we just kept going.

We had to feed the men, perhaps 10, 12 or more, lunch in the morning followed by the noon meal, & lunch in the afternoon. I'm not talking about tidbits here. Both lunches would mean stacks of sandwiches, usually a cake, and lots to drink, both hot and cold. We had to bake a second cake for the afternoon lunch because the first one would be completely eaten in the morning. Twelve hungry men can easily demolish a cake.

In addition to the food, we had to provide washing facilities for the men. They would be very dirty and sweaty as threshing was a hot and dusty job. To expedite the clean-up process, we would set up multiple basins, water, soap & towels on a bench or table in the yard. Fortunately, if all went well, it only took 2 or 3 days at any one farm. Rain, of course, caused delays.

LaVonne & I received so much pay for our dish washing efforts that we were able to purchase clamp on roller skates with our money. This was a good thing, as during favorable weather, roller skating was a popular recess activity at school.

That took care of the small grain harvest. Corn came later, usually after a hard freeze. Corn was picked by hand one ear at a time. The farmer would walk beside a wagon being pulled by a team of horses. The horses had no driver. The farmer just said "Giddy up" when he wanted them to move ahead a bit and "Whoa" when they were to stop. A hand shucker was worn in the palm of one hand and was used to remove the corn husk. The ear was then tossed into the wagon. A bang board was in place on the far side of the wagon, to prevent the ear from flying clear over the wagon. A farmer could get quite skilled at doing this and at times corn picking contests would be held. I know that my father entered at least once, and finished in second place. He said the first place winner did have a bigger load, but his was cleaner.

LaVonne and Norma on the front steps

Dad was more receptive to new things than most of the farmers around, and he, in partnership with Paul Burmeister, purchased the first combine in our county. Now the cut grain only needed to be placed in swathes, not shocked. My father took his binder and converted it into a swather to eliminate the cost of purchasing another piece of equipment.

The binder we had was a horse drawn piece of machinery, and it was also converted at this same time to be pulled by the tractor. This meant that my father could not make any adjustments to the swather sickle bar without getting off the tractor and walking back to it. If the swather was in need of frequent adjusting, i.e. the grain being down in places, he had LaVonne or me ride on the swather. He would then indicate by holding his fingers up or down, both direction and number of notches to be moved, and we would move the lever accordingly. We received a small salary for this duty also.

One day when LaVonne was riding on the swather my father noticed that she was getting very red in the face, and he felt she was suffering from the heat. He stopped and told her to go back to the house. She said, "No sir!" He then further stated that she would receive her pay regardless. She thought better of it and went in.

I remember singing and doing other antics while riding around on the swather and one day got my barefoot toe caught in a chain that stopped the whole machine. It could get dull for a little girl just riding around and around in a field!

I am helping Dad get the swather oiled and ready for use.

Getting back to the combine, my father and Paul sold this first combine and bought another, then repeated that at least one more time. He said they were always able to sell the combine for more than they had paid for it, as the demand was growing.

Many farmers were skeptical of the efficiency of the combine believing it was dropping an excessive amount of grain in the field. Some of them came to our farm to check this out for themselves. My father told them to go check the bottom of their straw stack. Plenty of grain was lying there, too.

We could climb up our windmill in late harvest time and count burning straw stacks, a very wasteful practice as straw made good bedding for livestock. There were no balers in our area that early. I used to enjoy doing this in the evening as I had no fear of climbing.

That first year, as soon as the snow had cleared out in the spring, we girls had a money making opportunity. The barn on this farm had burned down in 1935 and a new one erected. No one had bothered to pick up the nails that were left lying around the yard. We earned one penny per gallon syrup pail full of nails for providing this service. You could get a piece of candy or a balloon for a penny.

Later, LaVonne had been instructed in the proper and safe way to light the kitchen stove. We usually burned corn cobs and would sprinkle a small amount of kerosene over them to help get the fire started. One time no one was there when we arrived home from school. LaVonne lit the fire, but the flames leaped right into the tin can holding the kerosene. She ran quickly to the door and threw the can into a snow bank. It was revealed later that the truck driver, who made the fuel delivery, had mistakenly put gasoline in the kerosene barrel. Thanks to her quick action no harm came from this, but it could have been a disaster.

I don't remember when we first had a tractor, but I surely do remember using the horses. We had two Bay horses that matched in color, but one was a little larger than the other. My father was insistent that a team should be matched in both color & size as closely as possible. Prince was larger, and Dolly a bit smaller. Dolly was hyper and my father had to hold back on her rein all day until his arms would ache. For this reason, he did eventually sell her and replaced her with a roan colored horse whose name I can not even remember.

Prince was really cherished by my father and appreciated by all of us. He was very strong and very dependable. We had a 1938 Buick that we drove for a long time, and if it wouldn't start because of the cold weather, Prince would pull it backwards out of the driveway of the corn crib (which doubled as a garage at one point) to start it. Once during this procedure, Mother was leading Prince when she suddenly slipped on the ice and fell right in front of him. She was amazed and very grateful because he stopped instantly.

Also, my father would use Prince as a wind break when he had to go out in blizzards, to look for lost cattle or something. Gradually horse drawn equipment was replaced with machines pulled by tractors and there was no longer an economical reason to keep horses. The roan horse was sold, but my father couldn't sell Prince to just any one, or worse yet the glue factory. Finally, Prince was sold to Gordon Howe, a farmer in our area. Gordon was very fond of horses, and Prince was permitted to live out his remaining days in a comfortable, pleasant environment. Most farmers were strongly attached to their horses. I know of a few instances where farmers would be abusive to them, but that was rare.

My father grew corn, wheat, barley, oats & alfalfa at various times. During the war time he would grow a few acres of flax each year. The government encouraged the growing of flax then as the flax seed oil was needed for the war effort. Flax brought a good price, but was something of a gamble to grow as it could easily be wiped out by an unexpected frost and was especially susceptible to hail damage. Eventually the government offered a crop insurance program for flax, which is the first crop insurance program that I know of.

Dad also raised hogs to sell, and purchased cattle and sheep to fatten for market. We usually had one or two milk cows for our own milk supply and sold the cream in Chokio and/or traded it for butter. Part of the cream was used for our own cooking as no one worried about cholesterol in those days. Or needed to for that matter, as lack of exercise was not a problem. My Aunt Orva once told me that she felt like she couldn't cook if she didn't have cream on hand.

Once in awhile, LaVonne and I would be given the job of churning butter. This was not often, as we usually bought butter at the same time that we sold our cream at the Chokio Creamery. If we should run short however, butter could be churned by hand. We did not own a churn, but used a two quart fruit jar. LaVonne and I would be given this task, and would sit in the kitchen and shake the jar back and forth until butter was formed, maybe fifteen minutes. The contents would then be poured into a strainer and the liquid captured in another container while the butter remained in the strainer. The liquid was called buttermilk and could be drunk or used for baking, so that nothing was wasted. Mother would keep working with the butter until all the remaining liquid would be pressed out, and then shaped it into a loaf.

One year Dad had a sow that refused to accept her baby piglets, and he spent a long time working with her to calm her down to no avail. Our neighbor, George Kampmeier, had told my father that once when that had happened to him he became so angry with the sow that he struck her in the head rendering her unconscious. When the sow revived, she readily accepted the piglets. My father didn't want to do that, but what he did do was go to Morris and purchase some ether and anesthetize the sow. When the sow reawakened she accepted the piglets calmly and he had no further problems with her.

Mother raised chickens and geese. We always had down filled pillows in those days. Occasionally geese were given away or eaten for Christmas, but most were sold. At least once my parents sent a Christmas goose to James and Lucy Matchett of Chicago. Lucy is the daughter of Norton Jipson; Norton is the author of the Jepson Family genealogy book and a brother to my great grandfather, Norman Jipson.

Eggs from the geese were gathered by Mother and dated. She kept these in the pantry and rotated them everyday, so that one day the date was up and the next day the date was down. When she had collected several, they were then placed under a receptive goose hen for incubating until hatched. We did eat a few of the goose eggs, but not often.

One trouble that the geese caused was that during a rain storm they would sometimes run down the pavement eating the worms that had come out to enjoy the shower, or maybe to escape drowning. More than once Mother had to dash out in the rain to retrieve them.

There was one other problem with geese. They would attack during nesting season. My father had his leg bitten once by a gander, and he found that a rather painful experience. Geese were a minor enterprise for us, as we probably never had more than a dozen geese at a time.

The wing tip from a goose was used to keep the black iron kitchen stove top shinning and clean. There is just the tiniest amount of oil in the feathers which does the job. One additional perk from raising geese!

After we moved to the second farm, Mother didn't get back into raising geese. Chickens were another matter. Every spring Mother would order around 400 baby chicks from a hatchery in Missouri. One hundred of the chicks would be cockerels. They would be shipped by freight train and the depot agent would call when they arrived. Mother would have her brooder house & heater all ready to go.

The brooder house was on skids and was moved to a new location each year to reduce the likelihood of disease. The brooder stove had a large hood that measured maybe 4 ft. in diameter and burned kerosene.

The baby chicks would arrive in a large cardboard box with partitions dividing it into four equal sections (to reduce the possibility of them piling up during shipment) and had breathing holes small enough that the chicks could not get their heads stuck, but large enough to provide adequate ventilation. Each box held 100 chicks. They would be happily chirping away in spite of their long ride. You could hear them as soon as you walked into the depot.

We counted them as we unloaded them, and the hatchery would probably have put in a couple extra in each box in case some didn't survive the trip. Mostly they all arrived in good shape. Feed and water would be waiting for them, and they started to eat and drink immediately, followed by a quick dash under the brooder stove hood to warm themselves. It was always a happy upbeat experience to see and hear the new chicks. I don't remember what we paid for the pullet chicks, but the cockerels cost one penny each.

One year we had a visitor with a preschool child. My father took the child out to see the baby chicks. She said, "There's a million of them." He thought it was staggering even to contemplate one million baby chicks.

As soon as the roosters were large enough for us to eat, we would start using them and would later freeze any that we hadn't eaten. The chickens ran free in the farm yard and the meat had an excellent flavor as a result. As soon as the new pullets were laying eggs of sufficient quantity, we would start selling off the previous years hens. A few would be kept for making chicken & dumplings, chicken soup, & chicken casseroles. One could eat well on a farm and there was a certain satisfaction in being able to provide your own sustenance.

During the summer, when the chickens ran free in the yard, they would start roosting in the trees. As fall came on they would continue doing this as they did not realize that they should return to roosting in the hen house. Chickens would freeze to death in MN during the winter if left outside. Consequently, every fall we would have to go out in the dark after the chickens had gone to roost to gather them in. Once we started this procedure, the chicken house would be kept closed, so that the chickens were kept confined until the next spring. Lillian Benham tells me that they put chicken glasses on their hens at this same time. Confined chickens would sometimes start pecking at one chicken and once they saw blood they would keep pecking at that hen mercilessly. To prevent this, a small device called chicken glasses, but blinders would me more descriptive, was put on every hen. We never did this, and I do not remember having this problem.

The gathering in of the hens was sheer torture for me as I had a severe phobia of all birds. My father or mother would catch them and hand them to LaVonne or me. Our job was to carry them to the hen house. I would have at least two in each hand and held onto their legs with their heads hanging down. They would try to raise their heads up and peck my hands. I had to keep telling myself that "They can not reach my hands, they can not reach my hands" over and over. Thankfully, we at least did not have to apply glasses!

Every winter the previous year's hens would be culled out and sold at market as they would not produce eggs at the same rate as the younger hens. Most people were not too sentimental over this, but Hannah Burmeister told us that one year they sold their hens and then followed the truck all the way to Morris, which made her teary eyed. Hannah was an especially sweet person.

Chapter Three

Other Duties

Of course, Mother had a big vegetable garden and always had flowers. A row of lilac bushes extended the entire length on the south side of the house yard filling the whole area with its scent in the spring. A honeysuckle added to the aroma. This building site was located at the intersection of Highway 28 and a dirt road. In the ditch of the dirt road, there were several willow trees. My father would make whips and whistles out of the branches. I have always liked willow trees with their gracefulness, plus this nice memory.

There was a goldfish pond on this first farm, and during the winter the fish were brought into the basement and kept in large wash tubs. There were waterlilies, too, also brought in during the winter. Behind the pond and on the east side of the house were holly hocks, from which we girls would make dolls out of the blossoms on summer days. Those dolls had a very short life expectancy, but they were pretty while they lasted.

Summer also meant canning and later, after the locker plant was added to the creamery in Chokio, freezing. We never bought vegetables at all. Everything was raised, and enough was preserved to last through out the winter. If we didn't grow some vegetable, we just didn't eat that vegetable.

We didn't own a pressure cooker, so vegetables had to be processed by boiling on the stove for several hours. That was after being picked, washed, hulled, shelled or whatever was needed for that particular food item. We processed all vegetables except tomatoes in pint jars and they could be double stacked in the boiler. LaVonne & I supplied much of the manpower during the preparation by doing the shelling, washing, etc.

Mother always did the picking. She mostly didn't want anyone in her garden, but herself. Occasionally my father would stop off in the garden to do a little hoeing. When Mother saw that she would say, "Oh! He's in my garden" and dash out to protect her efforts. She knew he wouldn't damage any thing he recognized, but she worried that he would mistake some of her flowers for weeds, or step on something.

Some people did not bother canning peas as they said peas didn't keep well. We did, but we always wrapped the jars in newspaper which we tied securely in place with string, usually the string had been saved from the grocery store or meat market. My mother felt that helped to preserve them and ours did keep well with no problem.

In addition to the vegetables, Mother would purchase various fruits by the crate and preserve them. These, and the tomatoes, were processed in quart jars. Again, it would be enough to last all winter. Canned fruit was a common dessert for us, as it was for many rural people. My parents did buy fresh apples, oranges and bananas, which would be included in our school lunches.

There was one small apple tree on the first farm, but my father insisted that we never had one apple get ripe. LaVonne & I did like green apples. I do remember getting sick from them once.

Sewing was a given. We girls would look through the Montgomery Ward catalog and choose a dress style that we liked. Mother would then make the pattern by cutting the necessary pieces out of a newspaper free hand. Then proceed to make the dress. Patterns cost ten cents and she considered them unnecessary. Easter Sunday usually was an occasion for a new dress for each of us as well as one at the start of a new school year. All sewing was done on a treadle machine or by hand.

Mending was done to a considerable extent also. After our parents passed away, LaVonne & I found sheets that were patched, as that was their custom. There was no such thing as fitted sheets when we were growing up. Sheets wore out first in the center. They would then be cut down the center; the outside edges (which would be the least worn) were stitched together. Now the worn middle section was on the outside edges, and they would be trimmed to remove the most warn parts and hemmed. The resulting sheet would be too narrow to use as a bottom sheet, but would do for a top sheet.

Medical care seemed to be minimal in those days. We endured the whole range of childhood diseases, including scarlet fever, and rarely saw a doctor. A doctor was called for the scarlet fever, however. He put a quarantine sign on our house, and we could not go anywhere, and no one could come into our home. Neighbors brought any needed supplies and left them on the door step. Doris Kampmeier, our friend from across the road and a bit to the east, came to wave at us through the window. Bertha Davidson dropped off a book of

"*Gone With The Wind*" paper dolls. They were my delight; I especially liked playing with paper dolls, but had trouble getting other girls to play with me as long as I wanted to play. Now at the end of the quarantine period, our house had to be fumigated, and Mother thought it best to burn the paper dolls. I was heartbroken, but she was not to be dissuaded.

The only other time I remember seeing a doctor was after a few days with a sore throat, my parents called and I was scheduled for a tonsillectomy without the doctor even seeing me. This was performed in the doctor's office with the nurse giving the anesthesia (ether). I was home later that same day. The best thing about this procedure was that I could have a lot of ice cream.

Our mother did not seem to have as many obnoxious home remedies as some mothers did. She was a firm believer in Vicks Vapor Rub, and we were generously coated on chest & forehead as the occasion demanded. The only other treatment that I remember was flax seed poultice. This was homemade by mixing a small amount of ground flax seed in water and heating it. It was used to treat slivers that were difficult to remove. Mother said that the flax seed would draw the sliver toward the surface where we could remove it. It did seem to help.

Chapter Four

Our Town

Our town had a population of around 500 people. Most farms consisted of 160 acres, so there was a considerable rural population as well. We had 3 general merchandise stores (they did not sell meat which allowed a meat market to survive), two barbershops, a hardware store, a Gambles store, a blacksmith shop, a Chevrolet dealer, a Ford dealer, 3 farm implement dealers, a Great Northern depot, a bank, a lumber yard (which did not sell hardware as per an agreement with the hardware store to assure both businesses' survival), a jewelry repair shop (part-time business of a rural mail carrier), a telephone exchange, several grain elevators, a liquor store, a pool hall (men only visited this establishment, as ladies did not go into pool halls), a meat market, a beauty salon, a restaurant, a creamery where farmers brought eggs & cream to sell and the creamery in turn made butter to sell, a weekly newspaper, a post office, several gas stations, etc. Later, a locker plant & turkey processing business were added to the creamery, and my father worked there at times to help dress turkeys. He did the picking. We obviously could get much of what we needed right there in Chokio.

It was quite unusual for such a small town as Chokio to have a meat market. Ours was owned by the Ketter brothers. They did their own meat processing and everything was fresh and of top quality. People came from surrounding towns to buy their meat in Chokio. Even Morris residents drove over, especially if they were having company and wanted the very best meat. We would feel quite smug that Morris had nothing as good as our meat market. One unusual feature was seasoned hamburger. You could buy unseasoned hamburger or seasoned. My mother liked the seasoned the best as she said that she could not get it seasoned as well as they did.

My favorite store was A. J. Nelson Merchandise. Mr. Nelson was old, to my eyes at least, wore pince nez glasses and was incredibly kind. If we had a penny to spend, we would head to his store at noon time, where he patiently answered "How many of these do you get for a penny?" I mean over & over & over, & then probably again the next day, but he was always patient with us.

1946 sales slip from Nelson's store. Note non egotistical heading.

My father had A. J., as he was called, order a set of dishes for Mother the first Christmas (1937) we lived in Minnesota. It was a set of eight place settings plus serving pieces for a total cost of $5.00. I still have this set of dishes. They show a large arrangement of yellow flowers situated on a round table with a blue design.

At the store, coffee was ground on the spot. Bananas hung by the bunch, and the clerk would cut off the desired amount. Apples would often have worm holes and other defects, so customers would look them over to get the best ones possible. Vinegar came in a barrel & you brought your jug in to have it filled. We have a wooden vinegar pump today in our antique collection, as well as a couple of vinegar jugs. The grocer also bought eggs from farmers and some people referred to grocery shopping as trading.

These were our good dishes during the late 1930's and 1940's.

There were no shopping carts. You read your shopping list to the store clerk and he or she brought the item to the counter and bagged it there. Sales slips were written and tallied by hand. In addition to the food items, these stores also sold dry goods, such as sewing notions, overshoes, school supplies, and some clothing items; most of the clothing would be work clothes. It truly was general merchandise as advertised.

All of the stores were open on Saturday night and that was the time many people came to town to do their shopping. It thus created a social occasion for some as people stayed around to visit after the actual shopping was completed. We never did our shopping in the evening, but always during the daytime. Mother sang in the church choir and practice was on Saturday afternoon, so she did her shopping after practice and before returning home. Also, I suspect that my parents thought if we girls were allowed to hang around on the streets on Saturday nights, we might pick up some undesirable traits.

Most of the people living in the Chokio area were from families that were 1st or 2nd generation citizens. That is why people were so conscious of what nationality everyone else was. Most in and around Chokio were of German or Scandinavian descent. There were also quite a few Irish, as well as Polish families.

There was one man who was from Turkey, the only one in our community. His name was Solly Emit and he was widowed. His wife's two unmarried sisters lived with him. The sisters liked to raise ducks, but Solly didn't. One fall they sold all their ducks excepting two hens and a drake. During the winter, Solly hit one hen on the head killing it. The sisters felt so bad, but that did leave one pair. Later, the other hen suffered the same fate. Now they only had a drake, and he could be of no use, so they butchered the drake and ate him. However, it was all to no avail as, Solly said that the neighbors felt so sorry for the girls that they gave them "fifty-a more ducks." Solly returned to Turkey after his retirement.

One man named Frank Schott was from Germany where his father had been a cement contractor. Frank built a stone/concrete barn on his farm south of Chokio. It is worth seeing, if you are in the area, although the roof was destroyed in a storm. He designed and built cooling towers on all four corners as well as towers on both ends. These were designed to help keep the barn cool in summer. The stairs to the loft are also made of cement as is most of the interior. There is also a lot of cement work in Chokio done by this man. He had a very elaborate signature that he always put in his work. Later, he built a stone/cement house in Chokio where he and his wife lived out their last years.

Chapter Five

Early Friends and Neighbors

One of the first persons that I remember becoming acquainted with was DeWayne, better known as Dainey, Bennett. He was the son of the family who had rented the farm from Uncle Will Laughead. He was several years older than me and my father hired him from time to time to do some menial tasks. He undoubtedly had few useful pursuits in Chokio, so he would ride his bike out, as we were only a couple of miles east of town. He was probably kind to me, or at least tolerated me, and I developed a serious case of hero worship.

From time to time a fight would break out in the school yard, and a ring would quickly form around the event. Every time I would go running to see what was happening, and hoping against hope that Dainey would not be one of the participants, but he always was. I didn't speak to Dainey at school as I seemed to sense that he wouldn't want his tough guy image spoiled by anyone thinking that he was a friend to a little first grade girl. The Bennetts were nice people, but Dainey hadn't learned to control his temper. He eventually was expelled from high school, so he didn't graduate. He enlisted in the navy, and while there completed his high school studies and received his diploma. Whenever he came home he was sure to come to visit us. Our whole family liked him. After leaving the navy, he moved to Cutbank, Montana and worked in the mines, which were paying well at that time. When he returned from Montana for a visit, he was driving a big convertible. He continued to help out at our farm whenever he was in the area and was always dependable and fun to have around.

Once when Dainey and Mother were taking care of things at our place, our milk cow got into the alfalfa field and ate too much before we noticed her. This resulted in the cow bloating, a condition in which gases build up in the rumen, resulting in a mass of foam which prevents belching. The cow is thus stricken. A veterinarian was called and stabbed the cow with a trocar on the upper left side letting the gases escape. The exact spot was determined by placing his hand on the left hip bone and then reaching forward and down just a few inches. I was right there to watch during this procedure as anything to do with medicine interested me. The stench was horrible, but the relief to the cow was quickly evident. My memory of Dainey at this time was of his concern over the possible loss of our cow. It couldn't have been more pronounced if the cow had been his own, and it must have been a big relief to Mother not to have had the total responsibility for this event.

Dainey died in 1954 of leukemia. He was 28. I still miss him: he was like a big brother to me.

Another early acquaintance who stands out in my memory was Stanley Rilley. He had a corn sheller and was hired to come to the farm to shell corn. All corn was picked by the ear at that time. He must have paid some attention to me, as I always adored him and thought he was so handsome. Later, his son, Donald, was in my high school class. Donald married my good friend, Donna Twait, also a classmate.

Many years later, Stanley had a tragic ending. He and Donald were both working in the field, but a distance apart, when Donald noticed that his father's tractor had not moved for some time. When he went to investigate, he found his father on the ground. He had been run over by the huge rear dual wheels. Apparently, he had throttled his tractor down, and reached ahead to adjust something, lost his balance, fell in front the wheels and was run over. Because it was throttled so low, as the tractor dropped from his chest, the engine died. He was still alive when Donald reached him, and he was able to say, "That old tractor sure was heavy." Stanley died on the way to the hospital. Dad and I went to Chokio for the funeral; we were both living elsewhere by this time. What a tragic event for such a nice family.

Sadly, Donna died at age 60 from breast cancer. I still miss her, too. We had been friends all through school.

Grain for livestock was ground into meal. Bill Zentner owned a mobile grinder and came to our farm to do the grinding. On one occasion my father was in the grain bin shoveling grain into the grinder when he began to feel short of breath and weak. He was trying to use the scoop to knock open a small door near the top of the bin, when he lost consciousness and fell on his face. Bill wondered what was wrong when no grain was coming through and went to investigate. He found my father unconscious and drug him out doors, where the fresh air revived him. Apparently, the wind direction was such that the truck exhaust was blowing back into the grain bin. Another close call, but with no serious consequences!

My father complained of a headache, but never saw a doctor. In fact, my parents left that weekend on a short fishing trip with Paul & Hannah Burmeister and Ray & Evelyn Johnson.

Back row: Ray Johnson, Duane Jipson, Paul Burmeister
Front row: Edith Jipson, Evelyn Johnson Hannah Burmeister

Our closest neighbors were George and Edna Kampmeier and their daughter, Doris. Doris was a year younger than me and the three of us played together almost every day. We played house, of course, and played outside in the grove a lot. We also played with our dog, Tar, as he was always eager to be with us whatever we were doing. We had taught him to sit on one of our small chairs, where he would pose for us.

George was of German ancestry. He came over one day right after Germany had invaded Norway and said, "This war is getting very interesting over at our house." His wife was of Norwegian ancestry.

Tar posing on a chair circa 1941

LaVonne, Norma with Doris Kampmeier.
I was surely disgruntled about something.

George also advised LaVonne & me not to marry for money, but to love a rich fellow as you could marry more money in 5 minutes than you could earn in a lifetime.

Edna died young from cancer. George eventually remarried, but it was after I was gone from home and I never knew her. Doris still lives in Morris and Lillian Benham tells me that she recently had a call from Doris asking if she had read *"Dewey"* by Vicki Jipson Myron. Doris had recognized our family from the comments about my father near the end of the book.

Our neighbors to the west were the Karpinskys. This was a large family of Polish descent. They were wonderful people, would do anything for you and so humble. They only lived there one year after we arrived, then moved to another farm. They were renters, and at the discretion of the landlord could be evicted. March 1st was almost always moving day for farmers, as most of the previous years crops had been used or sold by that time. In this case the landlord wanted to rent to a relative. The Karpinskys stayed in the area and remained friends.

Many years later their daughter, Rose Mary, and I worked together at the hospital in Morris for a short time. She lived in a room near the hospital and I would give her a lift back to Chokio sometimes as she did not have a car. One morning, after the night shift, Rose Mary said that her mother & sister would be waiting for her to get home to feed the chickens. They would all go together to do that, and then the men in the family would see them and come to the chicken house too, as it was so much fun to watch the chickens eat. That's humble!

When winter set in, I decided to share Rose Mary's room. I worked the night shift and Rose Mary was on days. One day when she came home from work, she said she was going downtown to buy ice cream and asked how much did I want to eat, saying that she usually bought a quart as a pint was really not very much. Now, we did not have access to refrigeration so any ice cream had to be eaten when it was brought home. I said one dish would do me, so she came back with a quart and proceeded to eat the whole thing except for my one dish. The whole family had big appetites, but none were ever overweight, that I recall.

Rose Mary (who was a couple years my senior) had a lot of personality and was fun to be around. She had a comical way of expressing things. One that I remember is that she referred to some families in our area as "That Jones tribe", or "That Smith tribe". Those names are changed to protect the innocent. It never failed to make me smile. I'm not sure whether she meant that as a put-down or not.

South of us a mile lived the Rasmussens, Hans and Anna. They both came to the USA from Denmark. They had no children but a little dog and a canary.

The little dog had been taught to "lay down and woll over." They were very "old world" and spoke with a heavy brogue.

The kitchen on the first floor of their home was for show, and a second kitchen in the basement was used for cooking & washing dishes. This was a Danish custom. They ate in the basement when they were alone, but having guests meant running up and down stairs to serve the meal.

Hans owned a Caterpillar tractor and did some work for my father and others. Also, my father farmed his land at times. When we arrived in Minnesota the southern half of Stevens County had never been officially surveyed. My father and Hans both took jobs doing that to supplement their incomes.

Hans was very laid back and deliberate about everything he did. I do not remember ever seeing him hurry. My father on the other hand was always in a hurry and hustling every day to get as much done as possible. Hans would sometimes try to get him to slow down saying, "If I have nothing to do, that doesn't bother me."

Farmers usually sell their hens after the new crop of pullets are laying well. The reason for this is that as the hen ages her ability to produce eggs gradually decreases. Hence, the older she is the fewer eggs you will get from her. However, her appetite is undiminished and therefore the profit in keeping her is also lessened. One day Hans complained to my father that his hens weren't laying very well. Dad suggested that perhaps it would be good to cull out some of the older hens. Hans indignantly stated, "There's not a hen that is older then four years".

At one point Anna bought a male canary as she wanted to raise some canaries. She moved the bird cage into a darkened room and covered it over with a cloth, thereby creating a more "romantic" atmosphere for the birds. She asked my father if he thought that would be a satisfactory arrangement for them. I wonder if it didn't put the birds to sleep. I don't remember if they ever got any baby canaries.

Hans and Anna returned to Denmark for visits several times, always by ship. One trip was so rough that Anna lost several pounds, but Hans was never sea sick. One noon he, and one other man, were the only passengers who came to the dinning room for the meal. They moved back to Denmark in their retirement, but they shortly returned. They didn't like living there at all. The prices were too high, they didn't have any good music, and on & on. Their families were all in Denmark, but their friends were in Minnesota. They returned to the US and died of old age in Morris.

Chapter Six

Relatives, Visiting and Otherwise

Our only relatives in the area, in addition to Isabel's family, were the Laugheads; Uncle Will, Aunt Lil and their daughter, Gladys. Aunt Lil's full name was Lillian Bartlett Laughead. She was a sister to Isabel's mother, Myrta Bartlett Swann and also a sister to Sarah Bartlett Jipson, my great grandmother. So we were all cousins together. Uncle Will had been an industrious and capable person all of his life. Couple with that the extreme frugality of both him and Aunt Lil and you will not be surprised to learn that they had managed to accumulate a sum of money over the years. In our town, if the bank would not lend you money to buy a farm, you went to see Uncle Will. He helped many in the area to get a start, including my own father. Their daughter, Gladys carried on the policy after her parents were gone.

Gladys Laughead in her youth

Their frugality was carried through to the church affairs as well. It was said that even if Uncle Will was ill, he would be well enough to attend the annual church meeting to be present to vote "No" to any increase in the minister's salary.

Aunt Lil played the piano at church. One Sunday the minister requested a hymn to be played. Aunt Lil insisted that she misunderstood the number; in any case she played the wrong hymn. When she finished the minister said, "Mrs. Laughead will have her way at church as well as at home." She did have a reputation for wanting to be in charge and was rather a formidable woman.

Aunt Lil did all her canning in two qt. jars to save on lids, etc. For three people you can see you would have to eat the given vegetable for some time once it had been opened. Uncle Will said that Aunt Lil had patched his overalls so many times that people couldn't tell whether he was coming or going.

The Laugheads lived in a nice old Victorian home in Chokio. It was quite dark inside with heavy dark woodwork and heavy furniture. A mounted deer head hung in the front entranceway, which also contained an open stairway to the second floor. There was a fireplace in the dining room, but I never saw it used. LaVonne & I would stay with them when the roads were too bad during the school year. That was an experience. I remember that we were required to wipe our plates with a piece of bread to eliminate any possibility of waste.

Uncle Will was very stooped and walked with a cane. In his later years he became bedfast. A hospital bed was placed in the dining room near the bay window and we would visit him there. Aunt Lil had died a few years earlier. A cousin of Gladys', Nellie Erickson, came from Wisconsin to take care of him while Gladys taught. We girls would play Hearts with Uncle Will. He was unable to hold a handful of cards, so he would just leave his cards upside down on the bedspread without even looking at them. During the game he would turn over the corner of one card at a time until he found one of the correct suit, and the first one he found is the one that he played. Consequently, he made a lot of bad plays which sent us into giggles. He also lost a lot of games.

Gladys taught school in Chokio most of her working life. She was an excellent teacher, a good disciplinarian, and was always available to help any student in any grade, if requested. In my junior year of high school, Gladys directed our class play, as there seemed to be no one else available to do so. At this time she was the 7th and 8th grade teacher so this would not have been her normal responsibility.

Our first Christmases in Minnesota were spent with the Laugheads. Aunt Lil was renowned for her taffy making, and it was always sitting on the mantel in a small dish. We did not dare to ask for any, but we would be offered one piece after we had cleaned up our plates. Nothing could be wasted and children certainly should not be spoiled.

Otherwise the Christmas at their home was quiet and uneventful as far as we children were concerned, but we did not feel unloved. We always knew they cared about us and we were welcome in their home.

Aunt Lil's Taffy Candy Recipe

2 cups sugar
½ cup water
1/3 cup vinegar
Butter the size of a walnut

Cook the first three ingredients until it hairs good. Do not stir. Put into a pan and cool. When cool put butter on your hands and pull it until it is not shiny. Wrap in wax paper.

In later years, we had other closer relatives move to Minnesota and then all holiday dinner gatherings became a fun time spent with cousins. Darlene Jaeger, a first cousin, and I became fast friends and that friendship has lasted to this day. She was the cousin closest to me in age. She is now married to Rod Nielsen and they live in Arizona.

As small children, some of our gifts were homemade and others were purchased. We did spend considerable time with the Montgomery Ward toy catalog. One homemade gift that I remember was doll beds made from fruit crates, one for each of us. Mother had made mattresses, pillows, and quilts for the beds and Dad had made the beds.

Two photos of our favorite cousins
On the left photo: Darlene Jaeger, Janice Jaeger, Norma, LaVonne & Tar coming to get in the picture, but too late

On the right photo: Janice Jaeger, Norma, LaVonne & Darlene Jaeger

A birthday party for Janice Jaeger
Adults L to R: Grandfather Albert Jipson, Grandmother Effie Jipson,
Duane Jipson, Edith Jipson & Henry Jaeger
Children standing L to R: Janice Jaeger, Norma, LaVonne & Darlene Jaeger
Seated L to R: Dennis Jaeger & Dean Jaeger

Of course, we did have other relatives that came to visit occasionally. One was my great great uncle, Bill Crosby. He was a brother to my great grandfather, Richard Crosby. He would stop at our house to spend the night en route to visit his daughter who lived in Wadena, Minnesota. Uncle Bill was beyond a doubt the worst driver in our family. My great grandfather, Richard, was blind, so he did not drive. Bill had rolled cars over several times. One day while Richard was riding in the back seat, Uncle Bill lost control and said "We're going over Richard." The response from the back seat was "Just as if I don't know it."

No one was ever seriously injured by Uncle Bill's driving, but his daughter was pinned beneath the car once. Uncle Bill was a large and a strong man; he was able to lift the car off of her. The adrenalin must have been flowing.

Around the turn of the twentieth century Richard Crosby, my great grandfather, moved his entire family of ten people to Lewiston, Idaho except for my grandmother, Effie, as she was engaged to Albert Jipson, my grandfather. Her sister, Mabel Crosby James, also stayed in Iowa as she was already married to Oscar James. Richard moved back to Iowa after his wife died in the 1930's and lived with Effie and Albert Jipson, his last few years.

One amusing story that Richard told came about during an effort to convert the Indians in Idaho to Christianity circa 1900. At this time "fire and brimstone" sermons were the preferred theme to convince unbelievers of the error of their ways. Collections were taken up at any opportunity and maybe several in the same service. One evening at a revival meeting an Indian man seated next to Richard said," What's the matter with this Jesus Christ? Him all time broke."

Richard owned a pocket watch that he was very proud of, and people whose clocks had stopped would call some times to get the correct time. Having the correct time when alarm clocks were the only timepiece available could present a problem, if you forgot to do the winding. When we lived on the first farm in MN, our mail carrier was so punctual with his arrival that my parents more than once set the clock by him. Also, the telephone operator was called at times to request the correct time, assuming of course that your telephone was in working condition. Hopefully, her timepiece was accurate, or close enough.

Richard was also a source of medical advice which he shared with anyone who asked, and probably some who didn't. He had no medical training what so ever. After his blindness, he remained as independent as possible and when my father asked him once if he could find his bed, he stated, "If I can't, I'll spend all night trying." LaVonne and I, while still living in Iowa, were allowed to take his hand and lead him to the table. But, no help from anyone else, please!

Isabel Jipson's father, Ralph Swann, came to visit about once a year staying with Isabel. He usually remained for a length of time, weeks if not months. He lived in Wisconsin, and drove out alone. His driving skills weren't the best either, so it was always a worry. He lived with his son and daughter-in-law, Marion and Idy Swann, and would leave for Minnesota without even informing them. I guess that saved an argument. Isabel would be notified that he was missing from home and then she would expect him. He always arrived without incident.

When he came to our home for a meal, he often brought a large hunk of cheese with him. He kept eating off of one side and the back side would be positively green. LaVonne & I were turned off by that to say the least, but Uncle Ralph said, "By goll, this cheese gets better every day."

He drove very slowly in an old 1920's vintage type car, and often down the middle of the road. One day after a visit to our farm, his car wouldn't start. My father volunteered to push him in his vehicle with our car. I was riding along per usual. We had to turn one right angle corner and when we approached it my father told me that he was concerned we wouldn't have enough speed to get around the corner. And then Uncle Ralph hit his brakes!

Uncle Ralph Swann surrounded by my cousins, all Jaegers
From L to R: Shirley, Corrine, Sharon, Janice, and Phyllis

Uncle Ralph was quite hard of hearing and consequently spoke in a rather loud voice. He also said what he thought, as on one occasion at a wedding in the M. E. Church when I was a teenager. It was very warm and the church was full. I was seated next to Uncle Ralph, and as we were waiting for the ceremony to start, Uncle Ralph pointed at a large man seated a few rows ahead of us and said, "Too hot for that fat man." I was so embarrassed, and could say nothing, but just nodded my head as inconspicuously as possible.

When it was time for him to head back to Wisconsin, Isabel would be insistent that he go directly home, but he liked to go by the way of Iowa to visit relatives there. He told us one time "Isabel wants me to go straight home, but when I get out on the road I'll do as I've a mind to."

He continued to work on the farm with his son, until one day he suddenly died out in the hay field. Just the way he would have wanted to go. Busy and helping with his last breath!

Uncle Ralph's son, Marion Swann, was something of a contrast to his father. He would sometimes leave his field work and go down the road a short distance and sit in the one and only store in Attica, their town. He would visit and pass the time of day, with little care or thought about the work that was not being accomplished.

One day when a rain interrupted the work for all the farmers in the area, Marion went down the road a few miles to his cousin's farm, Blanche Jones and her husband. The Jones' were just in from weeding their fields by hand,

and Blanche made the remark that "The Lord is good to send us weeds to keep us busy and out of trouble." Marion's response was "Yeah, between the Lord, Dad, and Idy they got me going all the time." In telling the story later, Blanche added that it indeed took all three of them just to keep him going.

Another relative who brought joy whenever he visited was Uncle Ike Crosby. He was a younger brother of my grandmother, Effie Crosby Jipson, and the son of Richard Crosby. When I knew him, Uncle Ike had a filling station in Jordan Valley, Idaho. He displayed a sign that read "Last gas for 100 miles" and that was indeed the truth. Over his lifetime, however, he had worked at a wide variety of jobs including ranching, mining, prospecting, etc. Differences of opinion were often settled by fisticuffs and Uncle Ike being a large and strong man was called upon sometimes to come to the aid of someone else. It was still a case of frontier justice in many instances.

When he was a child growing up in Lewiston, Idaho, he was walking down the street one day, when a man came backing out of a saloon right in front of him, with a six shooter pointed back into the establishment. Not everything in Hollywood westerns is exaggerated.

He told of shooting rattlesnakes just outside his door. One neighbor drove a new car, but always in low gear. When asked why he didn't shift up a couple of gears, he replied, "No need to, plenty of power in low." He was full of good stories about the people in his area, referring to the cowboys as buckaroos. Neighbors lived a long distance away and you had to be self reliant to survive out there at that time.

Uncle Ike Crosby

Uncle Ike married a widow named Mamie, who had three daughters at the time of the marriage. His younger brother, Don Crosby, later married the oldest daughter, Mildred, making for an unusual relationship, as his brother was now also his son-in-law.

Visitors from my mother's family were more infrequent. Her brother, Bill Hill, did stay with us one summer. Bill was unmarried and had been in both WWI & WWII. This came about by his being drafted toward the end of the first war. He finished basic training and was sent to the Port of Embarkation when he contracted the influenza that was so prevalent then. By the time he recovered, the war had ended. When WWII came along, he had already developed a case of Parkinson's. He reported for a physical, as requested, and to everyone's surprise, he passed. He said, "Maybe I can do something that will relieve someone else to fight." He was shortly discharged, however, as he was not even able to complete the basic training.

The summer he stayed with us, he did build a yard fence that surrounded the house, garden & the flower beds. This project had taken on a sense of urgency when the cattle got out one day and ran between the clothes lines that held that week's laundry. My mother was not a happy camper that day as it all had to be done over. It took him all summer to build the fence, but he did a good & proper job.

Grandparents Maude and Alvin Hill and Mother's brother Bill Hill
LaVonne & Norma.

My father had erected new clothes lines when we first lived on the second farm. His technique was to dig a post hole and a trench of a couple feet or more in front of the hole. The post hole and trench were partially filled with cement containing scrap iron for reinforcement. This assured that even the heaviest load of clothes would not cause the post to lean forward.

He also designed the yard fence for easy plowing of the garden spot. The garden was to the east of the house. A narrow band of ground to the far eastern side was plowed initially, and then left undisturbed. This is where perennial flowers and herbs were planted as they wouldn't require annual tilling. Then the rest of the garden was next. At each end of this area, he used removable fencing, which could be opened up for plowing and tilling. To accomplish this, two posts were situated just an inch or two apart and were joined together by bolts that held them securely in place. One post did not go into the ground and could thus be swung away when required.

Uncle Bill loved baseball, so he fit right in; baseball being very popular in both our family and in Chokio. He attended all the games he could, even riding in with my boyfriend and me once. Uncle Bill returned to Iowa after that summer was over and lived with his parents until their deaths. After that, as his Parkinson's was progressing, he moved to the Iowa Old Soldiers Home in Marshalltown, Iowa. One of the main interests for the veterans at the home was the baseball games broadcast over the radio. Every game was discussed over & over again, thereby providing entertainment for days on end. He continued to live at the Old Soldiers Home in Marshalltown until his death in 1955.

My mother's one sister, Nellie Mayou, lived in Rosholt, SD. We visited her about once a year in the summer. She had a large family of ten children, and this is one case where the husband, Ed, did not help. She said she never got done; she just quit when she was too tired to go on. South Dakota can get hot and dry in the summer and Aunt Nellie had a large vegetable garden. She watered this by carrying five gallon pails of water out and carefully pouring water on each row. Her efforts were largely responsible for keeping this family fed.

Ed had a drinking problem and treated his family badly, being insulting & rude to all of them. The children would bring out their school papers, art work, etc. after he left for town, which was usually shortly after the noon meal. Then they would climb onto my father's lap and tell him things like they had a loose tooth and ask if he would pull it for them. They were really starved for a father's care and concern.

I often wondered why anyone as sweet as Aunt Nellie would marry someone like him, then one visit he was very polite and considerate to every one. If this was your only experience with the man you would have thought him the nicest man on earth. I was puzzled until it dawned on me that he was sober. The only time I saw him sober in my life. Such is the misery brought on by alcohol abuse.

My mother's oldest sister, Nettie and her husband, Lloyd Harner, lived on a farm near Dallas Center, Iowa. One time while visiting them, I went into the barn. There was a narrow passageway just in front of the horse stalls. The horses were busy eating their hay as I was passing through, when suddenly, without warning, one horse let out a giant sneeze just as I was directly in front of him. I was covered with partially masticated hay and other even less desirable secretions. The stench was horrible. I turned and ran back to the house, where I was subsequently denied admission. Aunt Nettie brought out a wash tub, I was stripped naked and bathed right there in the yard. A most unforgettable experience!

Aunt Nettie was an inveterate pieced quilt maker. She had seventeen nieces and each one of us received one of her quilts when we married. She had no children of her own. My mother also made quilts and gave one to each of her five granddaughters at the time of their marriage.

We were able to visit my father's parents in northwest Iowa periodically as the drive was about 200 miles. Part of the fun of those visits was my father's brother, Verlyn. He was 6 years older than me and always thought of fun things to do with us. One of our favorite things was the "Chicken Song". This was an original composition of Verlyn's. It consisted of him chording loudly on the piano and cackling like an old hen in a loud and sing song voice. We would laugh till we were crying over this. Verlyn just said that it stopped babies from crying.

If we could visit at the right time in summer, the mulberries would be ripe. To harvest these, my grandparents would spread old quilts and blankets on the ground. Verlyn was sent up the tree to shake the limbs causing the berries to fall. There would be holes in the old quilts and Grandpa said that we little girls could sit over the holes, spread our skirts out and eat any berries that fell on them. We liked that, of course.

My grandfather always called my grandmother Ma'am and never Effie which was her name. One time while driving up to MN to visit he said to her, "You watch for a while Ma'am as I'm getting tired." Surely he meant help me watch. My grandmother did not know how to drive and relied on her husband to take her wherever she needed to go. Although, she could manage a team of horse just fine, before cars came into vogue.

Other times our parents would make arrangements to meet our grandparents halfway to Iowa, in Montevideo or Redwood Falls, MN. Then LaVonne and I would be transferred over to go back with our grandparents, stay one week and then the procedure would be reversed.

One year we spent a week in Iowa with them during the M. E. Church's Vacation Bible School in Moneta. We were dutifully sent each day for our enlightenment. The first day the teacher read a Bible story, and when she finished she asked each student to draw a picture that would illustrate the story. Well, this presented me with a real dilemma as I had been day dreaming and had not the foggiest notion of what the story was about. I did this a lot. The most obvious solution was to watch what LaVonne was drawing, and copy that. When the pictures were collected the teacher went through them one by one, and commented. She just finished saying how happy she was to see the variety of the pictures, when mine came up next. I was so embarrassed and humiliated, too. You can be sure that I listened to the stories from then on.

I did have one redeeming moment before the week was out. The teacher read the story of the leper being repeatedly dipped into the Jordan River to affect a cure. I colored my paper completely with blue, and then drew concentric circles outward. The teacher said it was very original, which made me feel proud. I learned a valuable lesson about cheating, and as far as I can remember, I never cheated on any other assignment.

Driving down to Northwest Iowa became impossible after gas rationing. One time Dad and I rode down with a tanker truck. The driver dropped us off at Sheldon, Iowa about two o'clock in the morning. We didn't want to awaken my grandparents at that hour. My father said that the baker would be down shortly to open up. Sure enough around 3 am he unlocked his establishment, and he let us stay inside until Dad thought it was okay to call. I can't remember how we got back to Minnesota from that trip.

For us to visit my mother's family was more difficult. Mother, LaVonne and I took the train down to Des Moines, and we would be met there by her parents, who lived in Dallas Center, Iowa. This meant changing trains at the Union Station in St. Paul. I can remember sitting in the big waiting room, the red caps, and loud speakers calling out the trains. Rather a heady experience for two little country girls. I know we did this at least twice.

On the train and in the depot, we noticed people eating potato chips, and asked Mother to get some for us, but she always refused. I don't know if it was from a shortage of cash, or if she thought it would be messy. But what she told us was that we wouldn't like them. It was years before I got to taste potato chips.

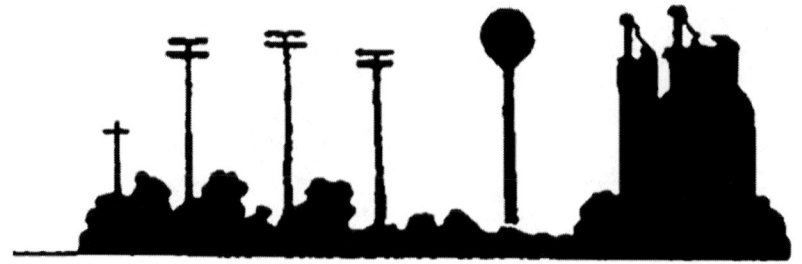

Chapter Seven

Church Friends and Activities

Another major source of early friends came from the Methodist Episcopal Church, as the United Methodist Church was called in those days. Some of those friends were Paul and Hannah Burmeister, Hank & Sophie Burmeister, Ray & Evelyn Johnson, Harold & Dorothy Johnson, Clarence & Doris Kahl, Emory & Bertha Davidson. Many of these had children near our age. It was customary to invite a family for Sunday dinner from time to time, and then they would reciprocate. This was one of our primary sources of socializing.

Chokio United Methodist Church, ca. 1940s

In no way could anyone in our congregation have been considered wealthy, but as for me, I wasn't so sure. There were two ladies who wore those small fox skins around their shoulders. I was fascinated by the little heads and the beady eyes on the foxes. I thought they must be very rich; this was surely the height of elegance.

We were the smallest congregation in Chokio. There were two Lutheran Churches, one for Germans, and one for Norwegians. These eventually merged to form one church, but that was after I had left the area. There was also a Roman Catholic Church.

The protestant churches women's organizations would put on dinners during the winter months. A nice evening meal (about 5 pm) would be served for a pittance, and the whole community would be invited. This was a primary source of revenue for the Ladies Aid, as the M. E. group was called. Mother and Ida Howe, whose husband bought Prince, were a team. This was fortunate as Mrs. Howe had a reputation for being one of the best cooks in the area. My mother was also a great cook, so they made a complimentary duo, and they usually drew a good sized crowd.

Twice a year, spring and fall, the women would meet at the church, and do an extensive cleaning. This included washing windows inside and out, as well as cleaning everything inside both the main floor and the basement. Even the more elderly women would come to help out. I suppose for all those who participated, it was an opportunity to visit with friends, as well as make a contribution to the church.

Rollie Bunnell served as the church custodian, and was responsible for ringing the bell 15 minutes before services, and again just before the church service started. Rollie's regular job was as town constable, but there was almost no crime, and people did not even lock their doors. As my mother said, "No one could bring you anything." The church had no bell when we first attended. It happened that my grandfather, Albert Jipson and his twin brother, Arthur, had purchased a farm on which an abandoned church building still stood. The church had a bell and he donated that bell to our church. The abandoned church also had a stained glass window and Verlyn tells me that that window was put into the barn on this farm. No one in our family seems to know what happened to the window after that.

To call Sunday school to order, the superintendent would strike a Burmese gong. This was a gift to the church from a missionary, who was married to one of the older Burmeister daughters (a sister to Paul), and serving in the Burma field. Our congregation would send them a contribution whenever they felt that they could. I'm sure it would have been a very small sum. My mother served as the Sunday School Treasurer for many years, and I remember helping her to count and put the coins in rolls, to be ready for deposit.

Christmas was a very special time at church. There was a large tree erected at the front of the church by the men, usually on a Saturday, and then the ladies would hang the lights, ornaments and red or silver rope. Gladys Laughead requested each year to be allowed to hand the tinsel. She did this after the others had left as she was very particular about the way the tinsel would hang. i.e. straight down. We always had a service on Christmas Eve, which consisted of the Sunday School children putting on a program. Near the end Santa Claus would arrive with brown paper bags of hard unwrapped candy, plus one piece of fruit, an apple or orange. Down at Nelson's store this same hard candy stood in open containers with a hand shovel for dispensing purposes. Candy was purchased by the pound back then.

When we first attended this church, there were no pews. The sanctuary was filled with individual chairs. The congregation was interested in acquiring pews, and was searching for some inexpensive used ones. The Ladies Aid received a letter from the Methodist Church in Janesville, Minnesota. They had had severe storm damage to their building, and were asking for donations. Our Ladies Aid decided to send them one dollar, and included in the letter was a statement that we were looking for pews. A thank you letter, received from the Janesville Church, mentioned that the owner of a theater there was trying to sell some old seats. A committee of Paul & Hannah Burmeister, Mrs. Les Spaulding, and my mother, Edith Jipson, was selected.

Paul, who had promised to drive, suddenly decided that he was free to go one day, and the others had no warning. When he picked up Mrs. Spaulding, she was just about ready to wash clothes, but laid that aside, and her husband, Les, gave her one dollar (the only money he had on him). My mother, also, had to hurriedly get ready, and my father had all of one dollar and a quarter, which he gave to Mother.

My mother did the negotiating for the purchase, and managed to get the price down from $125.00 to $100.00. The seats were in need of refinishing, but were sturdy. The whole group stayed overnight with a relative of the Burmeisters, with the three ladies sleeping in the same bed.

Paul wanted to go home by way of Minneapolis, and stop at the Montgomery Ward store. Mother bought a fishing lure for my father while there; Mrs. Spaulding saved her money. Thankfully, Paul paid for the meal, so the finances turned out to be sufficient.

The seats were refinished, and installed by all volunteer help, as most everything was in those days. They were short a few seats to fill the sanctuary, so some rows on the north side still had the chairs. Those seats served the church for many years until some real pews were purchased from the St. Cloud Men's Reformatory. The new pews had been made by the inmates in their wood working shop, and are still in service today.

In the summer, we would often attend Red Rock Bible Camp for a week. This was on Medicine Lake, just west of Minneapolis. Sometimes parents would drive us down in cars, and sometimes they hired a bus, depending on the number of people wanting to attend. This was a high point for us. The music was exceptional, and the services were uplifting and inspirational. On the weekends, many people would come out from the Twin Cities, and surrounding area. The crowd would really swell then, the sides of the tabernacle would be opened, and the sound of the music filled the whole area. The Hallelujah Chorus, from Handel's Messiah, was featured with the Sunday afternoon service each year. Beautiful!

A Galilean service was held on one evening, which meant taking several boats out on the lake. Those conducting the service would be in the boats, and the rest of us would sit on the shore. Of course, boating, swimming, etc was available any time.

Our church group at Red Rock Bible Camp circa 1947
Standing L to R: Edith Jipson, Mrs. Keeler, Marion Krosch, Doris Kahl,
Mary Cook, Mrs Braman, Bertha Davidson, Jim Graham, Isabel Graham,
Bonita Burmeister, Mildred Howe, Norma Jipson, Milo Johnson,
Lillian Jipson, Marvin Krosch, the bus driver
Kneeling L to R: Norma Severance, LaVonne Severance, Wilma Kahl,
Lois Radii, Jean Jipson, Ruby Schlattman, Emory Davidson

One happy memory of Bible Camp that I have is that I loved Fudgsicles and would buy one after the evening service, then walk so slowly back to my cabin that the Fudgsicle would be entirely eaten. Then, run back, and buy another one. Two always seemed to suffice.

Emory and Bertha Davidson were the parents of both Evelyn & Dorothy Johnson, and so were a generation older than my parents. Emory wanted some large rocks removed from his fields, and my father volunteered to help him by blasting them with dynamite. It was to be accomplished on a Sunday afternoon. When the noon meal was over, it was decided that the women would go along to watch.

The technique was to dig a hole under the rock, load it with dynamite, attach a fuse, light that, and then drive away to a safe distance. Now both Davidsons were short and very over weight. My father, on the other hand, had been a sprinter in high school running the 100 yard dash in ten seconds. Every thing went well for awhile, and then one time when my father jumped into the car to drive away, the car would not go into gear. This may have been a 1927 Buick, as I do remember that we drove one of those for several years. He put it into reverse; it wouldn't go there either. He said, "We'd better run for it," and they did. My father said when he got to the safe area, Mother & Emory were waiting for him, but he did manage to beat the old lady. Proving once again that proper motivation is the key to success! When, they looked back all four doors of the car stood open, and luckily the car was undamaged.

Bertha Davidson was especially dear to LaVonne and me. She was almost like another grandmother, always remembering our birthdays with cards and sometimes small gifts. I have a small porcelain cat attached to a smaller porcelain kitten which sits on a shelf in my kitchen to this day. This was a gift from Bertha and Emory Davidson.

Bertha died unexpectedly while I was in nurses training. Emory told me that it had gotten so that she would fix breakfast and do the dishes, then sit in a chair and sleep until he came in for the noon meal. That meal was followed by another period of sleeping in the chair until time for the evening meal. I suspect that she suffered from sleep apnea which no one understood at that time. I believe she was only around 59 years of age. Emory lived on into his 90's. As he got older he was unable to button his shirt sleeves as his hands were stiff and awkward. He would wait outside of church for some lady that he knew well and ask her to help him. My mother helped him many times. Emory would not feel it was proper to go into church without having his sleeves buttoned.

Ruth and Wilma Kahl (friends from Sunday School) were at our home one day playing. It was nearing Easter, and an exciting time for small children. Wilma was several years younger than the rest of us. She suddenly announced, "I don't believe in Santa Claus, but I believe in the Easter Bunny, cause Ma and Pa can't lay them eggs."

The Burmeister family, I'm speaking now of Paul's parents, consisted of thirteen children, plus the parents. When Paul was 4 years old, they moved via covered wagon and oxen to Oregon, where the father had purchased property. Unfortunately, no such property existed; they stayed awhile, and then moved back to the Midwest, ending up in Chokio. Paul was the oldest child who got to ride in the wagon, all of those older walked. As they went along, they would stop, and try to find some work to make a little money, and then move on. Once when they had no money left, Alma one of the older girls who was 12, found a fifty cent piece on the trail, and that was all they had. Alma was one of my Sunday school teachers, and a dear unselfish person. After the parents were gone, Alma managed the farm, and cared for a retarded brother, Emery.

Paul Burmeister
LaVonne, Ruth Kahl and Norma

Hannah Burmeister's family came from Sweden, and arrived in southern Minnesota too late to build a house before winter. They dug a hole in the ground, turned the wagon upside down over the hole, and lived in that the first winter. I do not know how many people this would have been. People tolerated some extreme conditions to try to get ahead. It was the Homestead Act passed in 1862 that prompted many of these families to emigrate from Europe. Some immigrants made statements like, "What a wonderful country, where they give farms away." Most could not have expected to ever own land in Europe.

These are some of the stories that LaVonne and I grew up hearing.

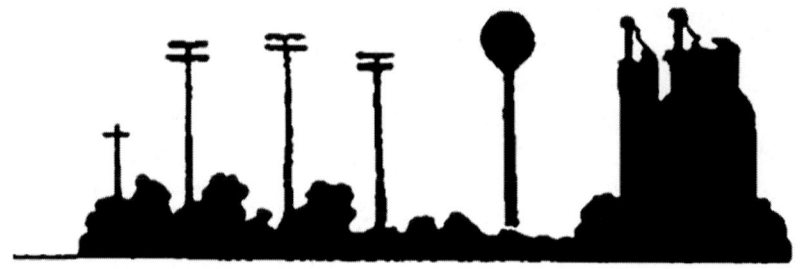

Chapter Eight

Extraneous Pursuits

LaVonne & I both participated in 4-H club, and took sewing and cooking, mostly. Mother and Dad both served as leaders at various times. The county fair provided the opportunity for us to exhibit our accomplishments, and each year we would show something. LaVonne was the county bread baking champion one year, and won a trip to the state fair in St. Paul.

The county fair, held in Morris, was a chance for everyone to meet, and associate with others from around the county, as well as take a break from the heavy work load. This was equally true of the children, who were in the 4-H program, as we competed, we also made friends. Of course, the county fair also meant fun and excitement for all of us. One year Mother entered the contest where you try to trip a mechanism by throwing a ball at a target, which, if successful, results in a man being dropped into a tank of water. She did so well at this that later, when we were just walking by the man started yelling, "Oh No! Not her again." We girls thought that was pretty funny.

Mother wanted me to win a trip to the state fair, too, but I was hopeless at bread baking. Trips to the state fair were also available for giving demonstrations, but there was a lot of competition for those. Mother thought that if I did a demonstration on health my chances would be better. There was a rule that at least one demonstration winner from each county had to deal with health. So, we came up with one, where I demonstrated bandaging. Since, I wanted to be a nurse even at that age that seemed like a natural. I did win a trip in this category, and Doris Kampmeier won in something, too. So, off we both went to the state fair in the big city all by ourselves. I think I was 11 years of age and Doris would have been 10.

We traveled by train, and were met by some 4-H people at the St. Paul Union Station. We stayed several days living in a dormitory on the upper floor of the 4-H building. One evening there was to be a banquet for all 4-H winners at the Radisson Hotel in Minneapolis. They were short of transportation, so it was announced that some of us would be taken in early, and were invited to Dayton's store to have cookies and lemonade, while waiting for the banquet. Of course, Doris and I volunteered for that. It is a nice memory to think of the cooperation, expense and trouble that some businesses were willing to contribute to be helpful for community events. We wandered all over the store, and I was surely impressed never before having been in a multistoried department store. We didn't buy anything on that visit, but I have repaid Daytons several times over the years.

When we returned by train, the first thing I told my parents was that I was starved. Since I still had money left, they wondered why. I said, "Doris was out of money, and couldn't buy anything to eat." Of course, I was too polite to eat in front of her. Dad asked why didn't I lend Doris some money, but I responded with, "I had all ready lent her ten cents."

Located in Morris was the West Central School of Agriculture. This was essentially a boarding high school, with heavy emphasis on Agriculture and Home Economics. An advantage to farmers in the area was that every summer they would hold an open house, and give a barbecue dinner. Field trips would be offered with explanations of the various crops, fertilizer, etc. on their test plots. The men could take these tours and the women could attend seminars on things of more interest to them. We participated in this several years. I believe that it ended with the start of WWII. This facility was eventually purchased by the University of Minnesota, and is now a part of the U of M Morris Campus.

The earliest pet that I had was a dog. While driving back from a visit to Iowa to see relatives, we spotted a sign advertising puppies for sale. A short drive off the highway brought us to the farm with the puppies. The man told us that they were wire-haired fox terrier pups, but they were obviously a mixed breed. We paid two dollars to the man, and the puppy was ours. I named him Tar, as he was mostly black with some white markings. This was probably 1939 or 1940, before gas rationing at any rate.

Tar was very intelligent, and we girls taught him several tricks. His most spectacular trick was jumping through a hoop. First, we taught him to jump over a saw-horse. We did this by one standing on each side of the saw-horse, and calling him to the opposite side. At first, he went under the saw-horse, and when that didn't earn a bite of hot dog, he tried to go around the end of the saw-horse, but that didn't bring the desired result either. We were indicating with arm motions for him to go over it, and as soon as he understood, and did it once, we gave him a bite of the hot dog. By the end of one hot dog, the trick was mastered. When, my father came in from the field for dinner, we proudly showed him the trick. He took an old tire, and cut a hoop from it. After that it was simply a matter of holding the hoop on top of the saw-horse, and over Tar went, and through the hoop. The next step was to take the saw-horse away, and the trick was learned. Sometimes my father would just make a hoop with his arms, and Tar would jump through them.

Norma with bicycle and Tar

His other tricks were less involved such as shaking hands, speaking on command, etc. I did try to teach him to climb a ladder once, but the rungs were not spaced appropriately for him, and it seemed to be dangerous for him to descend. So I gave that up. Tar would try to do whatever we asked of him, a very faithful pet.

Tar was either struck by a car, or at least grazed by a car one summer day, when he went out onto the highway. We did not actually see the incident, but he was missing a patch of hide three or four inches in diameter from his left flank. He spent a considerable amount of time just lying in the shade under the lilac bushes, where I would sit and stroke him for long periods. I was concerned because he kept licking the wound, but Mother said that was actually the treatment of choice for dogs, and would promote the healing. It did heal up nicely, and he never went near the highway again, thankfully.

My father and Paul Burmeister would tease Tar by giving him some food, and then placing their foot over it, so he could not eat it. He would get very scrappy and fight to get at it. They thought this was cute when he was small, but it wasn't as cute as he got older. We eventually had to watch him around some people that he just didn't seem to like. He never bit anyone, but would growl and snarl at them.

One evening, when I was a teenager, I was sitting on the floor playing with him as I had done so many times, when he suddenly attacked me, biting my left arm several times from my hand to mid-arm. My father used a rolled up newspaper to drive him off; he did not break the skin during this attack. The next day, when I came home from school, Tar had been shot, and was buried in the grove.

One very strange aspect of this is that Tar was extremely afraid of guns, to the point that he would cower under a bed during hunting season. My father said when he picked up his gun, he said "Come on, Tar" and the dog just walked out into the yard with him, and sat down waiting to be shot. I said he was very intelligent. Shortly before my father's death, he told me again how sorry he was that they had teased Tar. He was such a good pet except for that one problem.

My father, also, had an English springer spaniel for duck hunting purposes. His name was Belshazzer, but we simply called him Shazzie. Shazzie had the dog in the manger syndrome, which probably resulted from being the second dog in the family. He would eat or drink anything without hesitation. One day Mother sat a small can with a little kerosene in it down for just a moment and Shazzie drank some of it. She was quite concerned about what my father would say, as this was his hunting dog. Shazzie laid in the corner of the kitchen for a period of time and would draw his legs up as though to indicate a stomach ache. He did recover, however, and Mother said later that the dog did better and perhaps she had wormed him.

We also had a pet lamb for awhile. Paul Burmeister had a ewe that had given birth to triplets, and he gave LaVonne and me the smallest one to see if we could raise it. Well, the lamb thrived. He became something of a nuisance, as he was always right where you wanted to put your foot down next. You almost had to kick him out of the way. Sheep have a strong herding instinct because they are so vulnerable in the wild. I suspect that is why they try to stay right with you.

One day, Mother was going across the creek on stepping stones to feed the baby chicks in the brooder house on the other side. The creek was high, so she was watching her step closely, when she heard a splash behind her and knew that would be Shazzie, as spaniels love the water. Then, a second splash surprised her as Tar would walk around a puddle to avoid water. Finally, a third big splash compelled her to turn around, and there was the lamb, also swimming the creek. Stay with the herd whatever that required was his policy. They provided many hours of fun and amusement for all of us.

Norma and LaVonne with Shazzie and the lamb.
Note the fish pond and water lilies with the hollyhocks behind.

The lamb was eventually sold, probably, because we got tired of him always being under foot. Shazzie was given to Dainey Bennett by my father, I'm not sure why. Dainey came out one day shortly after that, and said that Shazzie now had something like ten puppies. On second thought, that may be what prompted the gift.

I mentioned earlier how we girls liked Fibber McGee & Molly. Radios were just as important to us then as televisions are today. Everyone had their favorite programs, and listened faithfully. Duffy's Tavern was a favorite of mine. They opened with the phone ringing, and a man's voice (Archie) saying, "Duffy's Tavern. Where the elite meet to eat. Duffy ain't here." This program had much the same format as "Cheers" did so many years later on TV. Of course, some shows were widely listened to like Jack Benny, Burns & Allen, Bob Hope, Eddie Cantor, and Fred Allen & on & on. These were popular with almost everyone.

We listened mostly to WDAY, the NBC affiliate out of Fargo, ND. A young Peggy Lee was a vocalist there for awhile. WCCO, the CBS station, in Mpls. was another popular station. Cedric Adams was on with the news at noon everyday. Our high school class was privileged to attend one of his broadcasts on a trip to Mpls. It amazed me that he could be so relaxed while reading at such a rapid pace, and speak so distinctly. Newscasters all read rapidly in those days. The listener had better pay close attention. At one point, he took off his glasses to clean them, and there was no break in the reading. He, also, wrote a daily column in the Mpls. Star Journal, to which we subscribed.

My father liked to listen for the market reports out of Chicago at noon. The announcer there would always end with "And it's a beautiful day in Chicago, and I hope it's even more beautiful wherever you are." In my mind, I can still hear that announcer saying that. It was uplifting, and conveyed a very real spirit of optimism.

The whole family enjoyed the beautiful music that could be brought right into our home by radio. The Bell Telephone Hour was a favorite. I thought that no one could sing "The Battle Hymn of the Republic" as well as Fred Warring and the Pennsylvanians, and that Kate Smith couldn't be topped singing "God Bless America." She, and countless other entertainers, spent many trips both abroad and in this country entertaining the troops. Bob Hope must surely have logged the most time and miles. We were proud of them all. Then, on New Year's Eve, it was Guy Lombardo and his Royal Canadians playing Auld Lang Syne that closed out one year, and welcomed in the next.

The 1940's were known as the era of the Big Band Sound. And their music remained popular for many years and can still be heard on recordings. The loss of Glenn Miller during the war saddened the whole nation. He was abroad on a trip to entertain the troops at the time.

I was never a fan of country western music as so many in our area were. I liked the popular music of the era, and knew the words to most of the songs. There was a magazine available that listed the words to the popular songs. We used to buy this sometimes. when we were in high school. We didn't want to not know the popular song words, if everyone else knew them.

After LaVonne went off to college I would frequently spend Sunday afternoons in my room listening to a symphony. I still like that music, too. Once, in Chokio, some local talent put on a minstrel show, my only experience with that type of entertainment. Improved sensitivity has put an end to this form of entertainment, as far as I know.

LaVonne and I were die-hard football fans of the U of M football team. even from our earliest days in MN. Every Saturday in the fall would find us one on each side of the radio, hanging on every word. Now there was no football in Chokio at this time, so we had never seen a game, but we could visualize everything. We had figured out what things meant like "fading back," "off side," "out of bounds," and horror of horrors "intercepted by" unless, of course, it was Minnesota who had done the intercepting. There's a red flag on the play always caused our anxiety to go up wondering if the penalty would be called against Minnesota or against their opponent.

Halsey Hall and Bernie Berman seemed like friends to us. Halsey was the announcer for WCCO and Bernie was the football coach. and we had unending confidence in them. Kenneth Hanks, a family friend, arrived at our home one Saturday just as we girls were bewailing a loss by Minnesota. Kenneth told us that the winning team was not a member of the Big Ten Conference, and we were somewhat consoled by that.

I have forgotten the names of the players from those earlier years, but I do remember the name Gordon Soltau, he would have been on the team in the late 1940's. Gordon was the kicker and we knew what it meant when he was being put in. I did go see a game while I lived in Mpls, and the program for the day had a large picture of him. Then later, while riding on a street car one day, I saw Gordon, and recognized him. Of course, I was too shy to speak to him.

My father enjoyed listening to the boxing matches, and I would listen with him. I was always cheering for Joe Lewis. I thought surely no one could defeat him. Shortly after WWII, a boxing match was arranged in Chokio, probably by some of the returning veterans. My father and I went. I didn't like it so well in person, especially as some of them were local men that I knew, and liked. I haven't felt the same about boxing since that.

At another time, the Harlem Globetrotters came to town, and played against some of our local players. I think we lost that one, but it illustrates again the community's enterprising spirit.

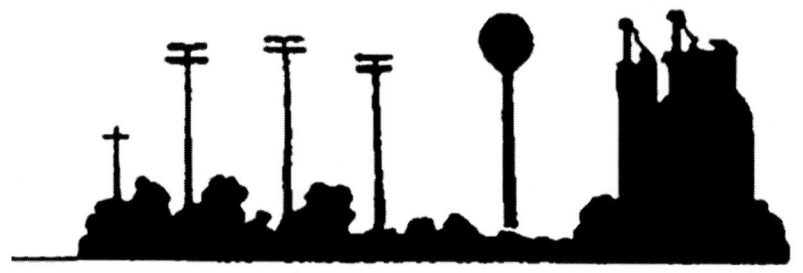

Chapter Nine

Sports

Other activities included hunting and fishing. Game was still plentiful at that time, and my father especially enjoyed it. Mother had a 410 shot gun, and she hunted some, but was more likely to be found at home cooking up something for the hunters to eat. My father had a 12 gauge shot gun, and a twenty-two rifle. He, also, had a Winchester 45/90, which was an old buffalo gun that he used for deer hunting. It was patented in 1886, and the internet states its value today is $2000 to $4000, depending on condition. My father lent it to our minister, and the man traded it for another gun. Apparently, he thought my father had given it to him. The minister said that it was too heavy to carry around.

At times, there would be organized fox hunts, usually after farmers had begun to complain of foxes killing their chickens. These were organized with a large group of men surrounding four contiguous sections of land. On a signal, all the men would walk toward the central intersection, and, hopefully, were driving the fox or foxes ahead of them. My father was a bit nervous about this technique, but I don't know of any serious problems that resulted to the men. It was bad news for the fox, however. The future effect of this was that the number of rabbits in the area increased dramatically in a short time. Gradually, the fox population would rebound, and then the process would be repeated. Today, my sympathies lie with the fox. They are a beautiful animal, and most chickens are no longer allowed to roam free. I hope fox hunts have ended.

One of Dad's best friends was Kenneth Hanks. He was the county agricultural agent, and lived in Morris. They hunted, fished and simply spent a lot of time together. Kenneth was single, probably a little younger than my father. He would be found sitting, and reading the paper in our living room many Sundays when we arrived home from church. Then he would stay through the afternoon. We were all fond of him and enjoyed his company: he became like family.

Joseph Grostephen, Hans Rasmussen, Duane Jipson with Norma, Hank Burmeister, Bonita Burmeister, Paul Burmeister

One year, before pheasant season Kenneth asked if it would be all right to invite a friend from Minneapolis to come for the hunt. Of course it was, and so began a long friendship with John Strait. John was also single, a graduate of Purdue University in Indiana and taught Agricultural Engineering as well as doing research, at the University of Minnesota, St. Paul campus. Being single, Kenneth was drafted early after Pearl Harbor, and was killed on D Day. He was buried in France, and a few years after the war, was re-interred at Fort Snelling. We drove to Fort Snelling to attend that service as did Kenneth's family.

At the re-internment service rifles were fired by the honor guard. I remember feeling very uncomfortable and unnerved by this. I know it was done in respect for his service to our country, but Kenneth was not a professional soldier: he was just one more young man who answered his countries' call. It didn't seem necessary to me.

On a lighter note, my grandparents, Albert & Effie Jipson, attended a similar service for someone they knew. When the volleys were fired off, the grandmother in this case fainted. One little boy shouted out, "THE SONS OF BITCHES SHOT GRANDMA."

John Strait called one year, and stated that he had married, and would it be all right if he brought his wife, Mary, along. She accompanied him annually after that, but never hunted. She was a delightful transplanted Texan, and Mother and she had a good time working together to feed everyone. One day, Mary told us that you should never ask people where they are from; if they are from Texas, they will tell you, if they are not, there is no use embarrassing them.

Pheasant hunting was in early fall, and deer hunting followed later. The group my father hunted with (it always included Ray Johnson and Paul Burmeister as well as several others), usually went north of Bemidji about 30 miles to a small community, called Nebish, to hunt for deer. Deer hunting trips were never undertaken without a planning session. The families involved would meet at one home, and the men would make the necessary plans. This would include all the wonderful tales of previous years' experiences, and adventures.

On one trip, I believe it may have been the first trip to the Nebish area, but I can't say for certain, the men arrived later than expected, as they had had some difficulties. It was dark; they were tired and unsure where to stop. They drove into a farm yard, and asked the people if they could sleep in the hay mow over night. The family insisted that they come in, fed them a good meal, and put them up in their own home for the night. The next morning, after feeding them breakfast, they stated that their son, Johnny, would go with them as a guide and helper.

On subsequent days, they met other neighbors in the area that also would hunt with them. The Mistic families (Pete, Jim & Tom) hunted with them a lot. These people were of Croatian origin, and very warm and generous. Hunting was more than sport for the men living in this area; it was a large part of the provisions for their families, as farming conditions here were marginal at best. To attend high school, which would have been in Bemidji, the students from the Nebish area would have to be on the bus by 6 to 6:30 am everyday, and of course, they were late getting home as well. You had to really want to go the school, and many did.

The men, especially Jim and Pete Mistic, became good friends, and later came to our area to hunt pheasants, and stayed at our home, as well as staying with the Johnsons and Burmeisters. Some years we would have quite a large group, I can't remember all the names. Even later, some of them had sons, who came down during harvest season, to get work wherever it was available. They would sleep in our hay mow, as there would be too many to accommodate in the house. Mother would feed them breakfast, at least.

During the deer hunting trip, the hunters would often travel to Red Lake Indian Reservation, which bordered Jim Mistic's farm. The Indians (these would be of the Chippewa or Ojibwa tribe) always had smoked white fish, which they would sell. That was a real delicacy to us.

One year, Paul shot a bear, and we were all invited to their home for a dinner of bear meat. Hannah, being a prudent hostess, also cooked some beef. Everyone ate bear the first time the platter was passed, but reverted to beef the second time around. The general consensus was that the bear meat had a sweet taste.

Fishing was something that could be enjoyed by the whole family, and one winter shortly after we arrived in Chokio, Dad and Ray Johnson built a boat in our barn. Boards were left soaking in the stock tank, until they were ready to be formed to the desired shape. We enjoyed that boat many years, and it would hold a lot of kids. This was important when we fished with the Johnsons, as they had four sons and a daughter.

Minnesota was a good place to fish. We caught walleyes, northern pikes, sunfish, croppies, both large & small mouth bass, & perch. Word about which lake was "hot" would get around, and then there would be a run on that lake.

We have rowed across Highway 28 when our creek flooded.
This is the boat that my father and Ray Johnson built.
Seated from L to R: Norma, LaVonne, Barbara Burmeister, Dad, Bonita, & Shirley Burmeister, & Hank Burmeister, Jr.

When our Iowa relatives came to visit, they always wanted to fish for bullheads. LaVonne & I didn't think much of that idea. Also, Mother got stuck with the cleaning of the bullheads. She had her own technique, which was to lay them on a tree stump, and drive a nail through their heads, thereby avoiding getting stuck by the thorns. Then, she would slit the skin on either side of the back bone, and using pliers pull the skin off removing the entrails in the same operation. She got quite fast at doing this.

On one fishing trip my father had caught a bass, but bass season was a few days in the future. He decided to keep the bass, and placed it in his tackle box. When they reached the shore, there was the game warden. Ray Johnson was holding the tackle box, and he was always ready and eager to tease someone. He kept making remarks about how heavy the tackle box was, but the game warden either didn't catch on or more likely let it pass.

On some fishing trips, Mother would take a one burner alcohol burning stove along with the necessary ingredients, dress out the fish, and we would eat them there, sometimes in the boat, or otherwise on the shore. Fish taste especially good when they are that fresh.

I remember one fishing expedition where our luck was phenomenal. We had just started trolling when the motor died, so we reeled our lines in. I had a red and while daredevil on my line, and I left it just touching the water. I was watching it wiggle back and forth, when suddenly a northern pike swam clear up to the surface, and grabbed it. Needless to say, that was an easy one to land. We knew we had a good fishing day ahead, and it was.

When, we went fishing with Paul & Hannah, Paul would always check the fishing barometer before he would consent to go. On one fishing trip with them, LaVonne dropped the stringer, which held several fish (the whole days catch) into the lake. She felt so bad. Paul, who had a lot of fishing equipment, gave her his grappling hook, and she kept working until, amazingly, she did retrieve the stringer with all the fish intact.

The boat was eventually given to Ray, and he in turn later gave it to his brother-in-law, who eventually allowed it to rot away.

A few incidental things about Paul. He wore a size 14 shoe, if anyone unfamiliar with this fact were visiting them, Paul would sit with his legs stretched out in front of him, stacked one foot on top of the other, and leave them there until someone commented. He also tried to get the chicken gizzard at picnics before I could, as we both liked that piece best. Paul had only a 4th grade education, but did a lot of reading, and served on the county agricultural committee as well as worked on various other community activities. He had managed to educate himself fairly well. My father always held him in high regard for his ability to hold his own with those around him.

One problem that Paul had was admitting when he was wrong. One year as he and my father were getting the combine ready for the harvest, some part on the under side was inaccessible. Dad said that my turning a gear on the top of the machine, it would rotate the desired part to a position where they could work on it. Paul said no, it wouldn't. Since it was impossible for either man to convince the other, they needed an arbitrator. Mother was enlisted. She had to crawl under the combine to observe and report on the effects of said turning. She stated that indeed the part did rotate to the required position. Paul's comment? "Well, we're both right."

Chokio had its share of team sports enthusiasts, and our whole family enjoyed the sports that were available. The high school had a boy's basketball team and a boy's baseball team. There were no competitive sports for girls offered, but the girls did have a tumbling team, which performed at halftime during basketball games, and of course cheer leading. In addition, adult men in the community would always have a baseball team that played during the summer months. We spent many Sunday afternoons watching our local team and cheering them on.

Chokio was the first town in our area to install lights on their ball field. This was in 1948, and was a big event for all baseball fans in the surrounding area. The eight towers were erected with all volunteer help. The first game under the lights was against Morris, whom we were always eager to defeat. That game drew a crowd of around 2000 people. Unfortunately, we lost, but it was still fun. I got so excited, and we were so crowded on the bleachers, that I knocked the root beer out of the hands of the man seated next to me. He took it in good spirit, and when the game was over he said, that if they had 1000 fans like me they would win every game. I still like baseball.

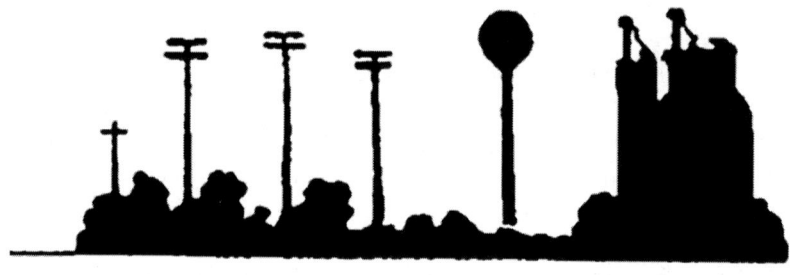

Chapter Ten

Hobbies and Interests

One summer a Baltimore Oriole built a nest in the tree near our back door. My father loved birds, and he would sometimes sit a few minutes on the back steps when it would be singing. He whistled the same notes back in response to the bird, and the oriole would answer. Eventually, he tried adding a note to the bird's normal song, and the bird answered back with the additional note included. The next year the bird was back, and they resumed their conversations. Finally, one year the oriole didn't return. My father took the nest into the school for all the students to see. It is a beautiful bird and they do make a very interesting hanging nest.

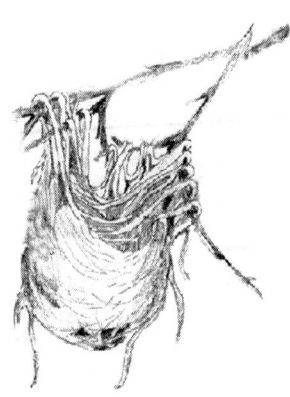

Baltimore Oriole Nest

His other bird project was to provide houses for martins wherever we lived, and he was always successful luring them into our yard. He enjoyed sitting out in the evening, and watching them sail overhead. That sailing was also beneficial as martins are renowned as mosquito eaters, a perennial problem in Minnesota. The houses had to be taken down, cleaned (sparrows would have occupied them after the martins left the previous fall), and put back up in time for the martin's arrival in the later half of April. If you were too early, the houses would be occupied by other less desirable birds, although the martins were capable of driving other birds out. Dad's house plans for the martins consisted of three stories with multiple apartments on each story. It came apart for cleaning purposes.

Another early memory is of my father reading poetry. He had kept his high school American Literature book, and liked to read out loud. I would sit on his lap as a child and listen as long as he would read. I can still quote from some of those poems after all these years. Mother and LaVonne would find some other activity, as they had little or no interest in poetry.

Probably, my mother's most passionate hobby was raising flowers. She planted a whole range of annuals in the garden every year and took a lot of pride in them. In addition, she maintained beds of perennials wherever she lived, until her very last years.

I can remember begging my mother to buy something for me to embroider, but she kept saying that I would not finish it. Articles stamped for embroidery, and, also, patterns you could stamp yourself using a hot iron were readily available in the 5 & 10 Cent Stores. These were all chain stores such as Woolworths, Kreskes (which has now evolved into K Mart) and Ben Franklin plus others. These stores served the same market as today's Dollar Store. She did finally relent, and purchased a tea towel with a tea pot stamped on it. I finished that, and have been embroidering ever since. Mother and LaVonne embroidered too and someone almost always had a project under way.

Many women made their dish towels out of 50 lb. flour sacks. Transfer patterns were readily available, and a common theme was to make one to represent each day of the week. We all made at least one set of those, I believe.

"Break Time"
2000 New Jersey
State Fair
2nd Place winner.

I still enjoy embroidery work; however, I require a magnifying light today. In 2000 I embroidered a picture entitled "Break Time" that my husband liked so much that he insisted that I enter it in the New Jersey State Fair; it did win second place.

Mother also made a lot of quilts. Most of her quilts were of the pieced and quilted type that is so familiar yet today. Hers were all pieced by hand and quilted by hand. These, of course, took many hours to complete and would be worked on for months. In the winter, the quilting frames might be set up in the living room for weeks on end, after the piecing had been finished.

If we needed a quilt in a hurry, she would turn to the tied quilt. This was done by attaching a cloth large enough for the lining of the project to the quilting frames. Then she would cover that with a thick batting, followed by a second cloth to cover everything. The layers would be tied together by using a bright colored heavy yarn and a darning needle. The ends of the yarn at each knot would be left about a half to three quarters of an inch long to add both color and design. This type of quilt could be completed in a couple of days and were very warm and quite attractive. We girls would help with the tying when we were around, but these were mostly done during the winter when we were in school. My father even got into the act sometimes and helped with the tying, too. We never had a purchased blanket of any type in my youth, Mother even made the bedspreads.

Mother also did a lot of crocheting, making doilies, tablecloths and afghans mostly. Hooked and braided area rugs were on our floors, all made by Mother.

LaVonne and I were both born with naturally straight hair and the time came when we wanted curls, after all many of our friends and classmates had curls. Leona Johnson owned and operated the beauty salon in Chokio. She was just beautiful, at least in my eyes. Also, her shop was the height of femininity, again in my eyes. It was divided into three stalls and all the walls and partitions were painted pink.

We girls were both taken in at the same time to get permanents. This was no small procedure. After the shampooing, small sections of hair were selected and a felt pad inserted over them to protect the scalp from the heat that was coming later. Above the felt pads a large heavy clamp was put over each wisp of hair, then the hair was wetted with a solution, rolled on a thin curler, and the curler was locked into the clamp. You were then seated under a machine with wires holding additional clamps hanging down. After each curler had been attached to a hanging clamp, the heat was turned on. This had to be endured for a period of time, until the beautician pronounced you "done". Styling came next, with an additional wetting, and curlers of some sort used. We were then seated under the dryer for the necessary time. The result was combed out and Wah LA you had curls.

There was no electricity on the first farm when we moved there and we were quick to sign up for that when it became available. The Rural Electrification Administration started installing it in our area about 1940. At first the lights would be flashed off momentarily at 9:45 pm each evening. Then, the generators were shut down for the night at 10 pm. It was assumed that everyone would be in bed by that time. REA customers at this time would only have lights; appliances came a little while later.

Signing up for electrification was optional. One man who decided against having it on his farm, told my father, "The first month you get a bill, you can't pay it. The second month you can't pay it, the third you can't pay it." Then, throwing both arms up into the air, he said, "PLOOEY! Your lights are gone."

After the move to the second farm, we were without electricity again, and it was back to kerosene lamps. Bernice Marquardt White, a friend and classmate, recently told me that when we were no longer going to have electricity, her family purchased our waffle iron for their use. To partially compensate for the lack of electricity, after the move, my father bought a Delco Plant. This was a generator that was placed in the basement, and would generate a 32 volt current. This at least provided lights, but no appliances. Electrification eventually reached us there, too, and after that my father had a bathroom installed complete with a septic tank connected to a drainage field. This farm had no creek to use for drainage.

Chapter Eleven

School Days

Mother would have made my dress

I started first grade in the fall of 1937. Miss Benson was my teacher. I was very shy, and was convinced that she had pets of which, I was not one. The superintendent and the president of the school board both had daughters in my class, and both daughters were pretty. I spent a lot of time day dreaming, and not listening. I remember that suddenly, I would realize that Miss Benson had given an assignment, and I had no idea what it was. I would, then, have to ask another classmate for the assignment.

One day Miss Benson read a story to the first grade class, while we were all seated in a semicircle. We were each given a book and instructed to turn to a given page, but not to look any further as the story had a surprise ending. I turned to the appropriate page, but no such story was found there. I tried to look a few pages before and a few pages after the correct page number. This brought a stern rebuke from Miss Benson. She looked at my book and realized that I had been given volume two. She then gave me volume one and the story was resumed, however, no apology was forth coming. Seventy years later, I still remember how hurt I was. I didn't do very well in first or second grade.

There was one memorable event, however. At Christmas we put on a show; the scene being Santa's workshop. Eight little girls wore crepe paper dresses made by their mothers. There were two each of four different colors. LaVonne & I each had one of these dresses, so our mother got to make two. In the show, we were wound up supposedly, & walked around stiff legged to the song "The Parade of the Wooden Soldiers." At the end of the song the winding gave out, and we all fell to one side on top of each other. Audrey Wensman's dress tore during the fall. After the curtain went down, the teacher tried to repair the damage, while at the same time trying to soothe Audrey's feelings and dry her tears.

In 3rd and 4th grade the teacher was Miss Laughlin. She was very stern and cross; she broke a lathe over the head of one boy one day. I was afraid of her and that didn't help. I seem to remember very little from these two grades.

5th & 6th grades brought me to Gladys Laughead's class, and for the first time I knew the teacher liked me, and I wasn't afraid of her. My school work began to improve, although, I do remember shedding a few tears over long division. Gladys's method for teaching this was to give us a series of problems. Then, she would walk around the class room, looking over your paper, and using a red pencil put a large check mark on the ones that were wrong. You then had to keep working those over and over until you got them right.

Gladys had another teaching method for improving our skills in using the alphabet. Every student had a dictionary, and when she called out a word, we were to find it as fast as possible, and then raise our hand. I did pretty well at that. Of course, she also taught the Palmer Method of Penmanship along with the usual array of other subjects. Gladys wrote a beautiful hand both on paper, and on the black board.

If we were in the receipt of a new textbook, which was an unusual occurrence, Gladys made each student open the book in a precise manner to assure that no damage came to the binding. The book was placed on our desks with the binding flat and all of the pages standing upright. We then put the covers down and pressed them with our hands. This was followed by putting down just a few pages and pressing again. We repeated this until all the pages had been pressed down. As you neared the center of the book, you could take more pages at a time. I still use this technique when I purchase a new book.

Fortunately, Gladys was moved to the 7th & 8th grades just in time for our class. What a blessing! By high school, I was as capable as the average child was to do well in school.

Our sophomore typing class. From L to R: Audrey Wensman, Leroy Diers, Bob Zentner, Donald Rilley, Wallace Theis, Norma Jipson, Bernice Marquart, Gordon Grossman, and Allen (Coke) Gillespie

One problem that schools all faced during the war was finding competent qualified teachers, especially schools in small towns. Spencer Klucas, the depot agent for the Great Northern Railroad, was enlisted to be the band director at one point, when no teacher on the staff was qualified to do that. Also, our school did not own a movie projector. Mr. Moffat, the owner of the Ford garage, would come to school whenever there was to be a movie, as he had a 16mm projector complete with sound. You can see that Chokio had a strong sense of community spirit and civic pride. Most residents did what they could to help out. It was 1947 before the staffing and equipment problems began to improve as GIs started returning and looking for employment.

During the depression, a new gymnasium had been built at our school using Work Project Administration labor. This was a Federal Government program to furnish work to unemployed people. An artist was employed, also WPA, to paint the stage back drops. Each class was allowed into the gym for a few minutes one time to watch him work. That was my first experience seeing an artist at work. Also of note, the Minnesota Historical Society has published a book entitled *The WPA Guide to Minnesota*. This is an excellent reference for anyone interested in Minnesota history, and/or planning a tour there.

Our school before the addition of the gymnasium.
The gym was added on the right in this picture.

After the move to the second farm, the bus ride was much longer, as we had more families to pick up. The bus could be very cold in the winter, as heat from the only heater would just reach the first row or two of seats. I decided to take a piece of slate that was meant to be used as a bed warmer. It was heated in the oven. and had a leather strap attached to carry it. I could put my feet on this. and they would be kept much warmer. LaVonne thought this was too embarrassing and humiliating at first, but eventually put her feet on it too.

One funny incident that happened on this route dealt with a family that only rode for one year. I have no idea where they came from, their name, or where they moved to, but they had 17 children. and thought anyone could farm. They had no previous farming experience, but had dreams of getting rich, I guess. This would have been during war time. One morning the bus stopped there and no one came out, the driver waited a period of time. and started to leave when one child came out of the house. The driver backed up to pick this child up, waited again. and then started to leave when a second child appeared. This was repeated at least once more. Finally, the driver said "Are any more coming?" One of children responded with, "Half of 'em aint't half et and half of 'em ain't half dressed." The driver elected to leave.

One good thing about the country one room school system was that on the opening day of school in 9th grade you had an influx of a lot more kids. Some I didn't even know, and others I knew from church, 4-H, or some other activity. Several of these stayed only a few weeks or months and then dropped out. What a shame!

One of the families whose children came into high school was the Hornings. They had a large family and two were in LaVonne's class. Dorothy became her best friend all though high school and they remained friends the rest of her life. Donald Horning became her steady boy friend, and they dated all through the last couple of years of high school and beyond. I believe this ended while I was in nurse's training, as I was not around at the time.

LaVonne's Engagement Photo

The break-up prompted LaVonne to move to Spencer, Iowa, to look for work there. Initially, she lived with our grandparents in Spencer. She eventually married Lowell Carlson, and stayed in the Spencer area the rest of her life. They successfully raised four children, who are now gone from home. Cancer claimed LaVonne in 2003, another one that is still very much missed.

I still keep in touch with Donald. Dorothy was also in my nursing training class at Fairview. She has recently lost her battle with colon cancer. Donald continues to live on his farm north of Chokio, and continues to help out the next generation during busy seasons. He is a history buff, and we enjoy visiting about that. Our parents became good friends with the Horning parents, Orville and Lillian, and that remained so the rest of their lives.

My boy friend in high school was Allen Gillespie, another product of the country schools. Everyone called him "Coke", a nickname he had acquired as a small child. We dated until I had been in nurses training for a period, and then he lost interest in me. Our dates were mainly movies and roller skating, but also county fairs, ice skating, etc in season. He died in 2002, and the last year or two of his life, we did converse on the phone. He had developed diabetes, and was on dialysis, a double amputee, blind & mostly house bound. He was a very fun person to be with, and even in his last years a phone call to him was enough to put a smile on your face. He told me on one occasion that when he got to be a junior in high school all the girls suddenly got a lot prettier. None of us know what we may have to face in the future. I often think of a quote that my grandmother used to say, "What can't be cured must be endured."

I had stated earlier that there was no crime to speak of in Chokio. Well, there was the case of the missing fruit. Hot lunches did not arrive in our school until after WWII. In the meantime, the brown paper bag was the conveyance of choice for lunches. We hung our coats and other wraps on hooks in the hall, and our lunches were placed on the shelf above. Students, who lived in town went home to eat; the rest of us ate out of our brown paper bags right at our desks. It occurred, suddenly, that various pieces of fruit and/or other goodies would be missing from some of the lunch bags. We didn't know who the culprits were, but the town kids were high on the suspect list. One of the perpetrators of this activity was exposed by Mickey Adolphson, who had laced an apple with red, hot pepper. That bit of low-tech investigative work managed to bring this crime wave to an abrupt halt.

In chemistry class, we were all seated at large laboratory tables. I sat off to one side. The boy to my left was not one of our more academically inclined scholars. Every day the instructor would start class with a ten question quiz covering the material that we were to have read. The questions were written on the blackboard, and this boy seated next to me would lay his textbook on his lap, out of the teacher's sight. He could get some answers by just thumbing through, and copying down the correct response. Well! One day, the instructor gave the questions orally. Now that presented quite a problem. Before he could find one answer, a new question was in the offing. He had quite a temper, and his face was getting redder and redder. I could see the frustration building. I was eventually overcome, and burst out laughing right in the middle of the test. That turned a few heads, I can tell you. And the offended party said, "Waal! Jipson." We had never been real friends anyway.

Thinking about chemistry class brings to mind another memorable incident. It was the class period in which we were to distill water. We were all given a collection of glass tubes and assorted other beakers, stoppers and so forth. I was somewhat less than skilled at heating and bending glass never having tried before; consequently nothing came out right or even straight, so that it was impossible to get a level apparatus assembled. Therefore, I compensated for this deficiency by putting a prop here and there to try to secure a state of equilibrium for the whole thing. What I succeeded in doing, of course, was constructing a veritable house of cards, which shortly collapsed. While I was down on the floor mopping and picking up things, I was hit by a shower of water. Elwood Johnson, who was seated on my right, was equally lacking in glass bending skills, and he had bent the glass tubing to the point that it was completely closed off. Unbeknownst to both Elwood and me pressure was building in his flask at an alarming rate; the stopper and contents were sent rocketing skyward which resulted in the water raining down on me. I let out a squeal. Rumor has it that teachers tend to go prematurely gray.

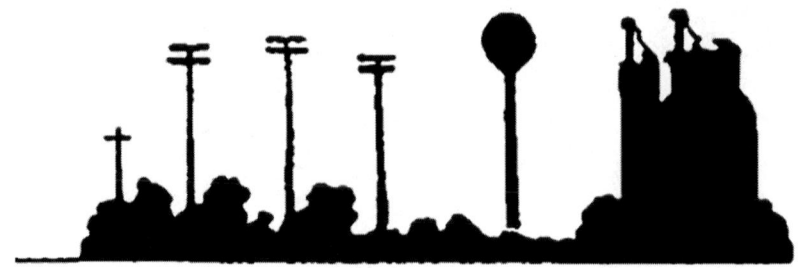

Chapter Twelve

Minnesota Winters

Winter could be a challenge in Minnesota. The Armistice Day (November 11th) storm in 1940 was talked about for a long time as one of the worst. The previous day had been a beautiful fall day and we didn't anticipate any problem. My father had all of his livestock secured except for the horses, and in the morning when he went out in the storm to do chores, the horses were nowhere to be found. He returned to the house after caring for the other livestock, and bundled up to go in search of them. He wore a long heavy sheepskin coat that had a large full round collar. Mother was able to tie this collar up around his head & neck with a scarf to keep the snow & ice out. He spent the greater part of the day searching, but could not find the horses. Toward evening, one mare came up to the barn. He was able to ride that horse back out into the fields again, and she took him to the other horses. All of our horses did survive, but some neighbors did lose horses in that storm, as well as other livestock. This would represent a severe loss during depressed times to say nothing of the suffering of the poor animals.

The 1940's seemed to have had a lot of winters with heavy snowfall. Out on the prairie the wind can do terrible things in a snow storm. As one man said, "There was nothing between here & Fargo to stop it." Actually, he could have made that the Rocky Mountains. Consequentially, the snow would pile into huge drifts. LaVonne & I could sit in a grain scoop with the handle out in front to steer, and ride down the drifts right in our yard. That was great fun. These same drifts had to be walked over, of course, to feed the chickens and other chores day after day. That was not so much fun.

When spring arrived the melting snow made for muddy yards. I used to enjoy making little streams and rivulets to help the water run off more quickly. Eventually, my father would use an old road grader to smooth all of the ruts out, and that would out put an end to my drainage systems.

The first farm we owned was located on Highway 28, the main road through that area. One storm my father went out to help stranded travelers so many times, and always came in with wet clothes, that he said one more time he would have to wear his good suit. We had his clothing hung up all over the house trying our best to get them dry. One stranded motorist was carrying the Minneapolis Sunday newspapers for delivery. In gratitude for the help, he gave us a free paper. My sister & I immediately began hoping that the baloney truck would get stuck. I never knew my father to take any monetary remuneration for helping people in distress. It was the "Golden Rule" in practice, or as one man put it "Try to see that everyone has a good day."

Our home on the second farm lay just west of two building sites that were directly opposite each other, both had good sized groves to provide wind breaks. Both groves were located adjacent to the road ditches. The snow would really pile in there. At least once the men in the community came to meet the snow plow with their shovels, and scooped the snow bank down to the level that the plow would be able to handle it.

In another incidence that I recall, my father was afraid we would be short of coal before the snow plow would get to us. Using Prince and Dolly, our only remaining horses, to pull the wagon he and I went to town. We took the most direct route, which meant going across fields and other people's property. He had wire cutters along and cut fences as needed. While he was getting the coal, I went to the school and got books and assignments for both LaVonne and me. The school was open and functioning to those who were able to attend. Then it was home again for Dad and me via the same route.

We had been home a short time, when we received a phone call from some Iowa relatives who had come up to visit, and asking my father to come into Chokio to get them. He had to refuse as the team was nearly exhausted; they had waded through snow that came up to their bellies in many places, while pulling the wagon load of coal. He did go in the next day to bring them out. Talk about bad timing for a visit. I suspect that the severity of this storm was not predicted by the weather bureau as I maintain that my father was not the type to be caught short of fuel, if he knew that a storm was imminent. Is it any wonder that Minnesotans are perennially glad to welcome spring?

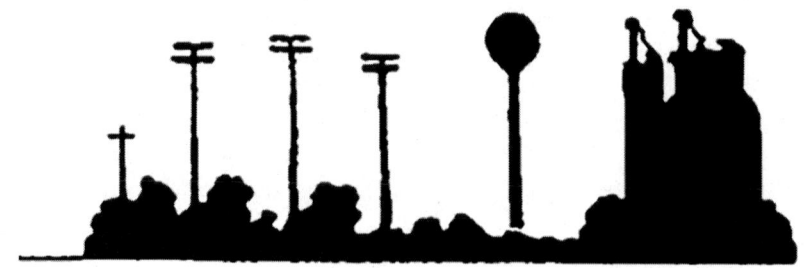

Chapter Thirteen

War

On December 7th, 1941 our life changed in many ways. It was a Sunday, and afternoon by the time we got the news. Kenneth Hanks was at our home, as he was so many Sundays. I remember earlier mentions by my parents of whether we would be able to stay out of this war. But basically, I was unconcerned being 10 years old. This news would have an ominous out come for Kenneth, as he did not survive D-Day.

Servicemen, whether enlisted or drafted were in for the duration of the war. There were no rotations back to the states. R & R to them meant back from the front lines a ways. My father had to register for the draft, but was given an agricultural deferment. Also, being thirty-one years old and with three dependents, he was past the age that was most apt to be drafted.

Some of the things that were rationed were gas, sugar, meat, and shoes. My parents followed the guide lines completely, but some people horded things they thought were about to be rationed. We never did, and we survived just fine. My parents did stop putting sugar in their coffee. Coffee was probably rationed, I don't remember. Things that had to be imported were generally in short supply due to the unavailability of ships. Bananas were mostly missing, and when a store managed to get some in, they disappeared quickly.

The sugar shortage also presented a problem with dessert making. Pies were a common dessert then, and ours all were home made. Mother came up with a recipe for Green Tomato Mincemeat Pie that she made repeatedly. I got very tired of that pie, and hope to never see another one. If you would like to try it, the recipe can be found on the internet. Also, candy companies were facing the same sugar shortage, and they came up with various substitutions. I will never forget candy bars made with soy beans. They were not very good.

When candy bars containing sugar were again available after the war, we school kids would go from store to store seeing who had managed to get some in. One day, in Henry Virnig's store I asked for two bars, Oh Henry! and Forever Yours. I was embarrassed, Henry Virnig was amused and all my friends had a good laugh.

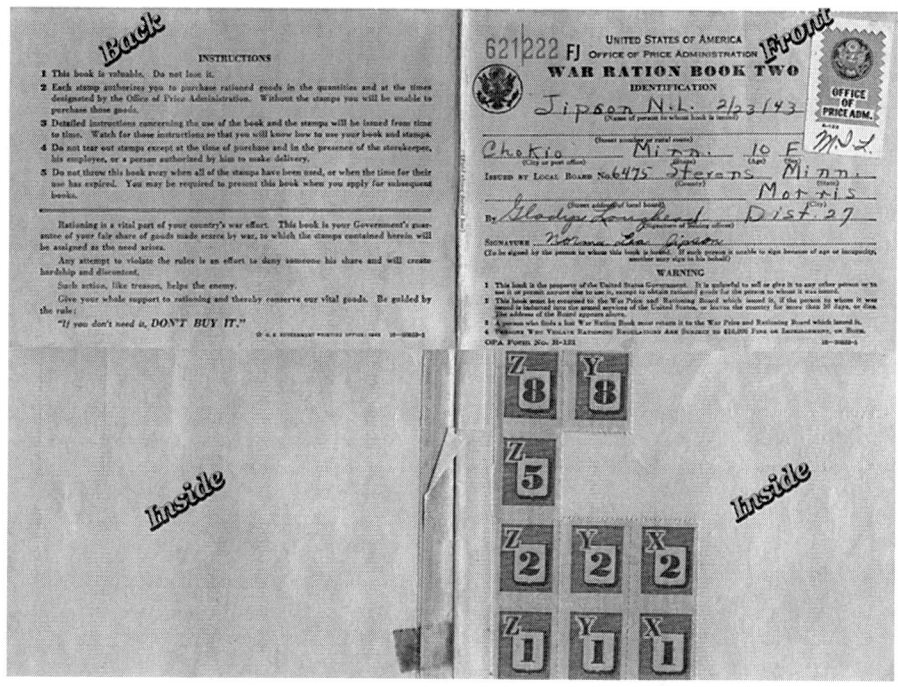

One of Norma's Ration Books Note Gladys' signature

Tires were just plain unavailable to civilians. Early on there was a requirement to turn in all unnecessary tires. You could have a tire on every wheel of every vehicle, but no spares. Every town had a big pile of used tires until they were all picked up. These were reprocessed, and made into new tires. The United States did have some plants that were engaged in making synthetic rubber, but not nearly enough. Tires, at this time, all used inner tubes which could and would be patched. The tires themselves were patched with something called a boot. Elmer Roan, an employee at the International Harvester business in Chokio, made a statement regarding one tire saying that, "It is booted to the very limit."

Metals were also collected, and turned in to be remade into war materials. Tin cans included. We were instructed to cut out both ends of the can, insert the ends into the can, and then smash them flat. These war time efforts were the earliest recycling that I was involved in.

Lumber was unavailable unless you submitted a plan that proved a real need, and explained how the proposed construction would help to increase production. Prior to WWII lumber had been dried naturally, now kilns had to be constructed, as we quickly used up the supply of naturally dried lumber. Lumber since that time is kiln dried for the most part. My father did secure permits multiple times, as he had several buildings constructed on the farm north of Chokio.

The production of autos for civilian use was stopped with only a few for the year 1942 produced, and then none were manufactured until 1946. We had the 38 Buick for a few years before, during & after the war. One benefit from the lack of new cars was that, in a town the size of Chokio, you had memorized everyone's car. One drive through Main Street and you knew who was in town, and if you wanted to see or talk to them you could.

One consequence of the gas rationing was a major increase in the use of public transportation. Both trains and buses were crowded and carried over the recommended limit of passengers. On one trip my father rode with three other men all of which were standing on the step just inside the bus door. The seats and aisles were already full.

Black outs were held periodically as practice in case of emergency. There was virtually no chance Chokio would be attacked, and my parents thought that this was done to keep the war effort front and center for people. My father was one of the wardens, and he had an arm band to wear, a flashlight to carry, and was instructed to drive around without using the lights on the car. He was responsible for a prescribed area, and was to make sure all lights were out.

We girls walked the road ditches to collect milk weed pods in season as they were used to fill life jackets. Posted on all hard surfaced roads were signs that read "Is this trip really necessary?" The speed limit was set at 35 mph, in an effort to conserve on gasoline.

Rallies were held around the country to raise money by selling war bonds. $18.75 would buy a $25.00 bond, and it matured in 10 years. We school children had books that we could paste stamps into. I believe one stamp cost a quarter, and when the book was full it could be turned in for a $25.00 bond. This was another job for the teacher. One day a week time was taken out of class, so any one wanting to purchase a stamp could. Teachers also were authorized to issue the ration books. The daily paper usually carried a map on the first page showing the position of the front. This was particularly concerning during the battle of the bulge.

Composers and lyricist did a fantastic job of producing music that was fitting for the country's mood. I can still remember the melodies and lyrics of many of the songs from that era.

> There'll be blue birds over the white cliffs of Dover
> Tomorrow when the world is free.
> There'll be love and laughter and peace ever after
> Tomorrow when the world is free.

Or in another beautiful song the words said,

> When the lights go on again all over the world,
> Then there'll be time for things
> Like wedding rings.

These were songs that tugged at your heart strings, and helped to keep people focused on what was really important.

Many years later, I learned what was important in North Platte, Nebraska. North Platte was located on the Union Pacific Railroad, and was a scheduled ten minute stop for troop trains. The residents of this town wanted to do something for the servicemen who traveled through there to show their love and concern for them as they headed off into harm's way. They turned their depot into a canteen, and met every train that came through with baskets of food and offers of friendship. This started on Christmas day 1941. Trains came through there starting at five am, and continued until after midnight every day. North Platte had about 12,000 people at that time, but they did get some help from neighboring towns. As many as 23 troop trains a day passed through North Platte, and as many as 8000 servicemen a day. This was strictly a local project; it had no federal funding. People cared. FDR did send $5.00.

As time went on, young men from our community were missing in action and some were lost. Eventually seven from Chokio were listed as killed or missing in action. That did not include Kenneth Hanks as he was from Morris. Adrian Karpinsky, our early neighbor and good friend, flying a B-24 Liberator over the Ploesti oil fields in Rumania, was one of those listed as missing and presumed killed. People with family members in the service had flags to hang in their windows. There was a star for each serviceman from that family, and a gold star for any one that had been killed.

In August 1945, the atomic bomb was dropped on Hiroshima, Japan followed in a few days by another one at Nagasaki, which quickly brought the war to an end. The Hiroshima attack caused my father to stay up most of the night reading the paper, and thinking of all the ramifications. That was the second night that the war caused my father to stay up most of the night. The other night that he couldn't sleep, was when we got the news that Kenneth Hanks had been killed. That night was for grieving.

I don't remember any celebrating when the war was over, just a profound sense of relief. There was a sense of elevated spirits when the veterans started to return. They added some color with their stories and their can do attitude. We were very thankful for all that had returned.

Chapter Fourteen

A Town Interlude

In 1943, my father unexpectedly sold our farm to the neighbor to the east of us, Bill Steuck. He never told me why he did that, but in talking to my cousin, Lillian Jipson Benham, recently, she said that he made an off hand remark to Bill that if he could get a certain price for the farm he would sell it, and Bill said, "I would pay that much." Since he had made that statement he felt that not to follow through would be dishonorable, and so the deal was done. I can't vouch for this, but it rings true as my father was very honest, and Bill Steuck would have had the necessary finances, as well as several sons, who would be needing farms.

He thought at the time we would move back to Iowa, but Mother was very opposed to that. Paul Burmeister got busy, and started looking for farms that were for sale. A true friend indeed! He found one north of town a few miles, which was purchased, and we had a place to move to.

One problem that resulted was that we had agreed to a March 1st move date on the first farm, and the new place was not available until November 1st. For those months, my father went to Moneta, Iowa and worked for various relatives in that area. Mother, LaVonne and I moved to an apartment in Chokio over the hardware store. LaVonne did go to Iowa a short time to help our aunt, Leona, with housework. I spent about a week living with the Harold Johnson family to take care of their three little children, while Dorothy went to the field to help Harold with harvesting. But mostly we were town kids for a change.

Mother got a job candling eggs at the creamery. Candling of eggs is done to insure a safe product to the consumer. The equipment consisted of a box shaped devise with a round hole smaller than an egg. The workroom was kept dimly lighted, and there was a light within the box. When the egg was held up to the hole, you could see if there were any defects within the egg, and it would be discarded if there were. The candler also sorted the eggs according to size; small, medium, large and jumbo. There was a scale if needed, but Mother told me that you soon learned to judge that for yourself. This would be the only time that my mother was employed off the farm. She usually had plenty to do, as you have probably guessed by now. One more thing about eggs. When we used our own supply on the farm, we never broke our eggs directly in with other ingredients, as these eggs had not been candled, and occasionally would have defects. Eggs were always broken open in a small bowl, and then added to the cake, fry pan, or whatever.

We did have a vegetable garden, as some new lots in Chokio were undeveloped, and they were made available to anyone wanting a garden spot. This was another thing that was being pushed all over the country during the war. Every one was encouraged to grow as much of their own food as possible. They were called Victory Gardens, and even appeared in most cities; including some in window boxes if that is all that was available to the family. One woman in Chokio planted all of her vegetables in V shape rows, but most people just tried to grow as much as they could.

There were not many children living close to the hardware store. Our favorites to play with were the Zismer girls, Norma Lou and Shirley. Shirley was in LaVonne's class, and Norma Lou was a couple years older. They were great pals, and we seemed to find things to do. Norma Lou was essentially a tom boy and a terrific athlete. She could whistle in such a way that she would be heard for blocks. She would give a whistle when they left their home, and we would be down at the bottom of the stairs by the time they reached our place. Then we would go off for ice cream cones or whatever.

They had a sad family history. The father had died early, and their mother passed away before we moved to town. I do remember being concerned about them at that time and asking my mother, "What will Norma Lou & Shirley do?" Mother said she thought that a neighbor of theirs would take the girls in, and that is exactly what happened. Such is life in a small town. Dear people! Norma Lou and Shirley did have two older brothers, but they were both in the military protecting their country.

LaVonne & Shirley were in the 8th grade at this time, and they along with Norma Lou had gone to a Sunday matinee at the theatre in Morris. When they came out, Shirley said she had something in her eye, but neither girl could see anything there. Monday in school Shirley had her eye bandaged, as it was red and watering. She was taken to the doctor, and eventually diagnosed with cancer of the eye. Treatment and surgery followed, but Shirley died, when they were in the 10th grade.

Shirley Zismer

The day of the funeral, we were snowed in as the snow plow had not gotten to us. After the chores were done, my father took his scoop shovel, and went down the road 1& 1/2 miles to a road that was plowed out. I don't mean that he shoveled all the way, but just where the drifts were across the road too deep to drive through. He thought that he would finish in time for him to go with us to the funeral, but it took so long, he had no time to eat or change his clothes. So, he drove us girls to the church, and then went down town to eat. I still get misty eyed over this story. Shirley was so pretty and so nice.

I called Norma Lou a couple years ago to see how she was doing. She lives in Morris, and is the only survivor in her family, as I am in mine. Norma Lou as I said was a tom boy, and an athlete. On field day, at the end of the school year, Norma Lou would be entered in the boy's events because she would win any girls' competition hands down. I can still remember the announcer calling out things like the winner of the boys 440 is Norma Lou Zismer.

In addition to track and field events, she was a good gymnast. One day in PE class, we were supposed to be practicing hand springs. Norma Lou was sitting it out on the bleachers. The teacher caller her out on this, and told her to do hand springs. Norma Lou got up, did continuous hand springs completely around the gym, and then sat back down. The teacher said no more. I have often wondered if she had had proper coaching and opportunity, whether she would have been Olympic material.

The other children, we played with, were Audrey and Gay Johnson. They were both younger than me. One Sunday morning while standing by the kitchen sink in my petticoat and skirt, Gay suddenly appeared at the screen door. Since it was warm the other inside door was open. Gay wanted to know if I would come out to ride bicycles with him. As I was getting ready to go to church, I said I couldn't. He said, "Could you if you had your blouse on?"

Audrey and Gay's mother was very talented with flower arranging and other crafts. She usually won several prizes at the annual flower show held in the Methodist Church basement. Yes, that was another thing that my mother helped with.

Their father owned fuel trucks & delivered gas, etc. to farms in the area. Audrey still lives in Chokio and is married to Jim Erickson, a boy from my high school class. Gay lives in Browns Valley, a town on the SD border. I don't know any more about him at this time.

Chapter Fifteen

Our New Farm

The building site on our new farm was back from the road about 100 yards, and two large cottonwood trees defined the driveway entrance. It was also larger at 280 acres. My father had his martin houses up in time for the bird's arrival, and a garden spot plowed for Mother before planting time.

An unusual feature on this place was that the original homestead claim shanty was still standing, although, it was in a poor state of repair. The Homestead Act, passed during the first Lincoln administration, stated that a structure for human habitation had to be constructed in the first five years on a land claim. The farmer had to live on the land for the five years, and make at least $500.00 worth of improvements. These were often just a small building called a "shanty". There were also a few acres on this farm surrounding a slough that was virgin prairie. This was cut for hay in late summer, but it provided a good place for wild life as it was undisturbed most of the year. Alas, it has since been plowed.

A third feature here was a country school house (now gone) which stood on the farthest southwest corner. One farm in a given area was chosen to furnish land for a school. There was no compensation to the farmer; he was expected to donate the ground. Each school had one acre for the building and play ground. This particular school had not been in use for some time. It seems that the school district was larger then most, and the number of children had become a problem. The solution was to pay a fee to the Chokio school district, and transport the students there.

The building was left standing because that allowed the school district to retain its status as separate from the town district. Demolition of the structure would have required the combination of the two districts and the resulting effect would have meant higher taxes for the rural district. Hence, the building was left standing empty; it was unlocked and some books and furnishing were still in place. We girls would go over to it once in awhile and look around, but never really played there, as we were older by this time. After a few years, as things started to deteriorate I did take a grade school book of Minnesota History. I still have the book and it makes a nice memory.

The move to the new farm meant new neighbors. A quarter mile to the east was a bachelor, named Lief Strom, with a housekeeper, Cora Hawkinson, & a hired man, whose name escapes me now. The strange thing was the hired man; he was so quiet and withdrawn, that he had not left the farm in years, and would not even wave at people. My father took it as a challenge to see if he could make the man wave. Every time my father would see the hired man in the field working he would wave to him, and after a long time, he finally waved back. One 4th of July my father came into the house on the run, and said for us all to look out the window. This hired man was driving his old 1920's car down the road. Dad said, "No one will be celebrating the 4th any more than that."

We bought our potato supply from this neighbor, as he raised several acres of potatoes, and my father did not like growing potatoes. An entire winter's supply would be purchased, and stored in a cool location in the basement. At least once during the winter, you would need to break off any sprouts that had developed. After I had started nurses training, Lief and his housekeeper, Cora, moved into Morris to retire.

The neighbors one mile north were the Adolphsons. There were several daughters and one son, in addition to the parents. One older daughter was married, and she and her husband lived there also. One snow storm our bus driver did not want to attempt the drive up to Adolphsons, and so dropped off four extra kids at our house. After awhile, we saw someone come walking down our road, and it was the married sister, Jeanette & Gene, her husband. They had gone to town for supplies, and were stuck in a snow drift. Now they had to stay the night also, and no one was at their home as the parents were away. They were very concerned about their livestock, as they had several milk cows. When cows are producing, they need to be milked twice a day without fail. My father thought it was too hazardous to try to reach their place yet that night, but the next morning, he and Gene started out across the fields using Prince as a wind break. They took along a wire cutter to cut fences as needed. The calves had burst out of their pen, and had nursed the cows, so things were not as bad as they had feared. A quick phone call to our home put the rest of the Adolphson family member's minds at ease.

A neighborhood card club was active in the winter. The game of choice was always whist, and a different family was host each time. Prizes were awarded (minimal) and lunch with much visiting. It was an effective way to pass some of the long Minnesota winter evenings.

The new farm also meant construction, as most of the buildings were in poor to fair condition. We moved the house to a new foundation and basement, and made some other improvements, like built in cupboards, new plaster & woodwork. Also, a coal burning furnace was installed with registers in all rooms, even upstairs. No more cold bedrooms! All of this was done before we moved in. The old basement, which was one half the size of the house and had a dirt floor, was filled with rocks, and used as a drainage field. Also, a new barn quickly went up, followed by a corn crib, machine shed & chicken house. Being wartime all of this required permission from a county board to purchase the lumber; as I've said before.

The carpenters, who were employed to do the construction, were John Hilla & his sons from Donnelly, Minnesota. John came to the US from Poland, and was the hardest working man I ever knew, and drove his men just as hard. When he arrived in Manhattan just off the ship, one of the first things he saw was a hole being dug for one more skyscraper. John went right over there, and applied for a job. There are many stories about this family. If John felt a worker was not giving his all, he would yell "Get to work or I'll kill you." To people like my father, who was always working hard, he would say "Go a little faster, if you can." My father worked with the Hillas whenever farm work would allow him some time to do so. He liked the man, and always respected him, as he worked harder than anyone.

Whenever they were working for us, my father would tell Mother to bring out coffee in midmorning. John would protest saying," Don't bring coffee." Mother listened to her husband, so she brought out coffee, and always something to eat with it. John would take a cup, tip it up and drink it down without stopping. It didn't seem to matter how hot the coffee was. He did allow the others to finish their cup, but then, it was back to work.

His one son, Ray, told Dad that once John fell from the peak of a barn, which they were shingling, all the way to the ground. The son started to scramble down to him, when John raised his head up, and told him to get back to work. Ray said his father laid there a while, and then got up and drove home.

Buck Hilla, one of the sons, was reportedly the fastest worker of the lot. He was laying a wooden floor in our back porch one day, and I determined to find out how he could do it so much faster that any one else. Here's the secret. My father was cutting the boards, and putting them in place ahead of Buck. Buck was nailing the boards, and his hammer never stopped the rhythm, as one nail was finished he struck the sub floor just ahead one time, and by the next swing of the hammer, he had the new nail in position to be pounded. The rhythm of the hammer was never broken. Buck must have used this same technique to nail shingles. People sometimes placed bets on how long it would take him to shingle a given roof. The person to lay the shingles for him had to be carefully chosen, as many men could not lay shingles, and move out of his way fast enough for him.

One summer, John bid on a government construction job. Every town in the farming areas of the US had multiple steel grain bins used to store government purchased grain. This time, the government had chosen to use wooden buildings. And John had the low bid. He stopped at our home, and asked my father to help. His plan was to use all his usual employees as foremen, and hire high school and college students to do the actual carpentry. My father said he would, but he was not happy about it, telling Mother that he would be spending all of his time just keeping them working and not wasting time. When he got home after the first day of the project, he had a smile on his face. He said that John walked up and down between the rows of bins hollering "Get to work or I'll kill you." That solved any discipline problems before they could arise.

That family is all gone from the area now, and the last I knew of them the youngest son had a construction company in a suburb of Minneapolis.

As time went by, my father made some other smaller improvements to help the work go easier and life more pleasant. An addition for summer time comfort was a fifty-five gallon open drum that was placed in the windmill tower. This, when filled with water, was heated by the sun, and a hose led into the claim shanty, where a shower head had been installed. We could all get a shower, if no one used too much water. Showers had to be short.

Later, an old pop cooler was purchased, and placed in a small structure that had replaced the claim shanty, and was located close to the well. The windmill, like most in the rural areas, would have been wind driven. The plumbing directed the water first through the cooler, then into the stock tank. This meant that whenever water was being pumped, the cooler was refreshed, keeping cream and milk cool, and also, cases of soft drinks were put in for hot summer days. We girls would stop in there and hold our hands in the cool water for a few minutes on really hot days. You could cool yourself down very nicely doing that, the only problem was that it was short lived relief.

A small stock tank, made from one half of a wooden barrel, was put into the barn by laying a pipe line from the large outdoor tank to this smaller indoor tank. The indoor tank was a few inches higher than the outside tank, thus preventing any water from running over inside the barn. This improvement occurred after an experience Mother and I had. My father was hospitalized, and she and I were doing the chores. It was winter, and bitter cold with a strong wind. The milk cow had recently had a calf, and was producing a lot of milk. We had to drive her out to drink, but this cow refused to go out the door once she felt the blast from the wind. After multiple tries by both of us, Mother said for me to carry pails of water to her. Well, she kept drinking and drinking and drinking. When she finally had her fill, she was so cold from the icy water that she was trembling all over.

Many times over the years, Dad had asked Mother if she didn't want to get a new gas range for cooking. She was adamant in her refusal. Her reasoning went like this. She knew how to cook on this old stove, she said. Besides the far side of the stove top, away from the fire box, was useful to keep food warm in case my father should ever be late coming in for the noon meal. My father never carried a watch, and he never varied more than a few minutes from noon, but then you couldn't be certain. Farmers got almost as good at reading the sky as sailors. Also, we would lose the reservoir of nice warm water for washing hands. Then again, that far side of the stove was used to make cottage cheese. Mother would put a pan of whole milk on the stove top's far side, and leave it there until it was well curdled. Then, it was strained through a cheese cloth to remove the whey, seasoned, and a small amount of fresh milk was added for moisture. It was as good as any cottage cheese you can buy today.

One very hot summer day in 1948, my father walked into the kitchen at noon time and said, "This does it, we're getting a new stove." Mother had been canning all morning with the wood stove burning steadily for several hours. The kitchen was nearly unbearable. A new gas range was quickly purchased, with my father not even going back to the field, but rather drove to Morris, and accomplished the deed before Mother could change her mind. Mother was soon adept at putting out the meals, and other things, as good as ever.

After electricity was available here, the windmill was no longer needed. Dad was not looking forward to taking it down, as it would be quite a chore, and hazardous to boot. One very windy day, we came home from Morris to find the windmill lying on the ground. No damage was done to other structures, and the hardest part of the demolition had been accomplished by Mother Nature. A real stroke of luck! These structures could become hazardous as they aged. We were lucky all right.

Mrs. Keeler, a sweet elderly lady who attended our church, walked out to turn off the windmill one day on her farm, after she noticed it appeared to be wobbling. The entire wheel came off just as she got to it, and struck her, breaking her back. She was widowed and was not found until later that day, when her son came by. She survived that and lived several more years, faithfully attending church every Sunday. Her picture will be found on the Bible Camp photo.

By this time my father had his own grinder, a stationary model, which he positioned in front of the barn, and extended the blower to reach into the hay mow. He built a small bin up there with an opening in one corner that led to the first floor. A small corner bin directly below received that part of the ground grain that could drop down as the bin filled. This meant that a small scoop and a few steps would deliver the feed to the milk cows. My father used to feed a combination of oats and corn ground together: he wanted all the animals to be well fed, so never skimped on that. As the quantity of grain in the hay mow bin diminished, we did have to go up, and push the feed toward the opening from time to time. Still it was a labor saving device, and made a useful storage area for the ground grain.

Barn photo showing the grinder blower pipe extending up into the hay mow

We had four or five milk cows by the time we girls were in high school, and the whole family knew how to milk cows by hand. LaVonne and I had all the cows named, and they all had their own personalities. The most extreme one for being slow was Peggy. She was quiet, and moved at a very deliberate pace. She was the last one out the barn door no matter if you released her stanchion first or last. At the other end, Long Legs was nervous and excitable. She certainly didn't want anyone out before her. We used to leave her last to be released sometimes, just to watch her maneuver. She wanted to be first! She could be quite rude pushing the other cows out of her way. Not unlike some people I've met.

Long Legs, also, liked to jump over the fence at certain times, and frequently injured a teat or two in the process. When this happened the chore of milking her fell to my father, as she could make good use of those long legs.

One evening during, one of these milking sessions, our two little neighbor boys were visiting, and telling us all kinds of little boy things, while we milked. When Long Legs started in to kick, the boys looked startled, and then, my father told them that this was the cow that jumped over the moon. Well! Their eyes did grow big, and they got back clear across the aisle from the cows.

The only protection that I know of when a cow is prone to kicking is placing kicking chains on her hind legs. This consists of a pair of J shaped brackets that were placed on her ankles, connected together by a chain. The cow could only move her hind legs a short distance once these were in place. However, sometimes the cow would jiggle her legs up and down in rapid sequence, trying to shake the chains loose. Beware that you get them securely placed!

Bag Balm was used to promote the healing of the injuries to teats, as well as chapped udders. Cows that lay on damp and /or muddy ground to any extent could develop severely chapped udders. Severely chapped teats could also produce some pretty spectacular kicking. This was frequently a problem in the spring, when the ground would be cold and wet, for a length of time. Bag Balm was also used, by many farmers, for human skin problems, and is still available today. This was purchased from traveling salespersons as they traveled their rounds throughout the rural areas at that time. There were two competing companies that I recall, Raleighs and Watkins. My mother often bought vanilla from these companies, as well as a soft drink mix, that was sweetened, and used much like Kool Aid is today.

LaVonne and I went upstairs one evening to go to bed, while our parents were saying goodbye to some visitors out in the yard. We, suddenly, spotted something on the wall over the door to the hall. LaVonne jumped into bed, covered her head over, and ordered me to go get help. I went out and told our parents that something was in our room. My father took a fly swatter and a rope, saying that if it was as big as I was saying he would need the rope, if it was as big as he thought, he would need the fly swatter. Well, he was surprised because, it was a bat. He picked it up with some clothing to protect his hands, and released it outdoors. We never did figure out how it got into our house.

Another story that pertains to invasive creatures involves bees. The house on this farm had a swarm of bees living just under the roof on the northeast corner. At first, they didn't really bother any one, but after a few years they seemed to get more vicious for some unknown reason. It got so bad that you could be walking across the yard and a bee would swoop down, and sting you with no provocation. It was really awful when they got into your hair. My father decided we had to get rid of them one way or another. He removed a few lathes in the area where the bees were living, and used an old vacuum cleaner to draw them in. We did succeed, but not before we were all stung multiple times. I seemed to react to the stings worse then the rest of the family with a ridiculous amount of swelling. To this day, I try to avoid bees whenever possible. We had no idea that people could have serious anaphylactic reactions to bee stings. That vacuum cleaner was history, if anyone is wondering.

When my parents moved from this farm, it was purchased by Leo and Lillian Benham. Lillian tells me now that the bees did return, and they subsequently swarmed several times. Harley Peters, a local bee keeper, came each time and removed them, making both parties happy. Harley was married to Ruth Kahl, our long time friend from Sunday school.

I went along with my father one day to get a load of hay off an area of virgin sod on a farm to the west of ours. This was about 160 acres that had never been plowed. The grass had been cut, and put into stacks. I was romping around on top of one stack, when I suddenly let out a scream. Now several people had reported seeing a bear in the area, which would have been pretty unusual, but not impossible. Any way, my father came running up the stack with his pitchfork in front thinking he was going to have to fight a bear with the fork. I said, "I saw a mouse." He was so disgusted with me that I don't think I have ever screamed at a mouse since.

My father had a plan to make haying less work and go faster. He took an old car, reversed the clutch, brake, etc. then, built and attached a giant fork like device to what had been the rear of the car. After the hay was mowed and raked into swathes, my mother would drive this device, called a hay bucker, and pick up one sling full of hay at a time. She then drove it to the front of the barn, where LaVonne & I would have laid three ropes on the ground. Once Mother had the load positioned over the ropes, we both stood on the loose hay with pitchforks holding back the hay, while she slowly backed off, and then left to get another load. The three ropes would then be brought up together by us girls, and attached to the pulley system, creating a sling. The pulley system consisted of a large rope which ran from the ground in front, up to the hay mow door at the peak of the barn, where it engaged into a trolley mechanism, the trolley traveled completely through the length of the hay mow on a track, and the rope only extended down to the ground on the back side of the barn. After the sling was created, I would run to the back of the barn, and drive a tractor positioned there and attached to the large rope by a clevis. As I drove the tractor forward, the sling full of hay was lifted into the hay mow. My father was located in the hay mow, and when the hay arrived at the position he wanted, he would give a yell, and LaVonne would pull the trip rope releasing the hay. My father, using a pitch fork, would spread the hay in the mow in a manner that made it as easy as possible to remove the hay when it was needed. This was called mowing the hay. If the hay was left helter skelter it would be very difficult to pull loose at feeding time. Once the hay had been released, I would back the tractor up to be ready for the next load, while LaVonne was retrieving the trolley mechanism, and replacing the sling ropes in position on the ground. I returned to the front of the barn, and we were ready for the next load. This was quite efficient, and as you can see required the services of the entire family, but represented a big reduction in the overall work load.

Newly invented hay bucker with Dad and Paul Burmeister

Dad & Bertha Davidson with loaded hay bucker

Most farmers at this time walked beside a hay wagon, pulled by horses or a tractor, and with pitchforks threw the loose hay one forkful at a time onto the hay rack. The farmer would have placed one set of sling ropes on the floor of the hay rack. When the rack was about 1/3rd full, they would place the second set of sling ropes, and repeat that later for the third sling set. One hay rack of hay would contain three slings of hay, when it was full. This was not only hard hot work, but time consuming. The hay had to be mowed twice, once on the rack and again in the hay mow. The load was driven to the barn, where it was unloaded using the same kind of pulley system as ours. This was a much slower process.

Another story about haying involves my driving the tractor behind the barn. The large rope had broken a couple of times, and Dad had spliced it, so it was short. I had to back up precisely in order to position the clevis directly over the pulley, or it wouldn't reach low enough in the front to allow for the creation of the sling. This was not difficult, because you have perfect visibility (the tractor did not have a cab), and when you do one procedure over and over you do tend to get rather good at it. One year, my father had told a neighbor, Alvin Lange, he could have half of our slough hay, if he would put it all up. He, also, told him to come to the house to get me, and I would drive the tractor behind the barn for him. Well, on the first load Alvin called back to me asking if I could back it up a little better to give them more rope in front. I said, "No." He said all right, and shortly appeared behind the barn thinking, he would be able to back it up better himself. When he looked at the situation he just said, "Oh," and went back to the front. He did go around for awhile telling people what a good tractor driver I was.

One year, this same slough hay land was rented to another man, who was not a farmer, but rented a building site only. He was rather a ne'er-do-well, and did a little of this and a little of that, and not much of anything. But he did have a milk cow, so it was agreed that he would put up the hay on halves. His method was to make several small stacks right in the field. One day, during the following winter, one of his small sons told my father that "All of our stacks are gone and some of yours."

This same man asked my parents one year, shortly before Christmas, if we would allow them to hide two children's sleds on our farm. This represented exceptionally expensive gifts for this family, who were of rather poor circumstances. They would be gone a few hours on Christmas Eve, and we were to deliver the sleds, and put them under the tree. My parents added a few other things, and some candy to make it as special a Christmas as possible.

As we girls were getting older, our help out jobs got more strenuous. We walked the corn fields to pull weeds that the cultivator had missed. Also, we were sent out with a tractor and wagon to pick up small rocks. On the first such venture, LaVonne said she would pick up all the rocks if I would do the driving. She soon changed her mind on that idea.

Large rocks would be removed with a tractor and log chain, after being dug loose. My father handled that, but I was right there if I wasn't in school. I thought it was exciting when big rocks were dug out of the ground.

One of our least favorite jobs was kicking corn back in the crib. Ear corn was sent up a grain elevator, and fell into the crib, but as the crib got full we girls would be sent up to kick the corn and/or try to direct it to the back of the crib with a sheet of metal. This could be quite strenuous, and seemed to reach that stage in the evening and into the night. We would fall asleep on the corn between loads and would only wake up when the corn started to hit that metal sheet. That was loud! Periodically, my father would come up to see how full the crib was, and then he would say, "Oh, I think we can get another couple of loads in here." Corn that did not fit into the crib would have to be stored out of doors, where it would not keep as well. Frequently after a particularly hard days work, my father would say, "Well, we didn't do very much today, but we'll really give it heck tomorrow." This would be followed by groans from my sister and me.

I remember one year when the harvest season had been so wet that the corn just was not dry enough to keep well. Also, the yield was large enough that it could not all fit into the corn crib. My father built some temporary cribs standing in the yard out of snow fencing material. During the winter he had a man come with a loader and move the corn from one crib to another in an attempt to aerate the corn. This is what prompted the construction of a second corn crib larger than the first crib.

My father, Orville Horning, & Fred Fischer were the township trustees for Everglade Township. One of their duties was to see that the roads under township care were properly maintained. At this time, some roads were under township care, some under county care and some under state care. They consistently had a problem getting gravel for the township roads. There was a farm in Everglade Township that had a gravel pit, but the owner lived out of state, and they seemed to have trouble getting a response from him. One of the men came up with the idea of trying to buy the farm. The owner was agreeable to this, and so it was done.

The buildings on this farm consisted mainly of a house and a barn. There was a couple from Scotland, the McKenzies, living in the house, and they were allowed to live there rent free, if they would watch that no one stole gravel. This had happened sometimes under the previous owner. This pair had a delightful Scottish brogue and referred to LaVonne and me as the lassies. My father was amused by Mrs. McKenzie one day. He mentioned to her that the paper had an article stating that rations were being cut again in Great Britain. She replied, "And the tay, did you notice the tay. Why the poor souls will have hardly a taste."

A decision was made to tear the barn down, probably for tax reduction purposes, as there was no livestock on the farm, and the barn was old and in poor repair. The chore of the barn demolition fell to the three families, since our family had no boys guess who got to go and help. The Hornings had 4 boys and the Fischer's had 2. Teddy Horning, the youngest boy and I were given the job of pulling the nails out of the siding boards, after the uprights had been removed by more mature & capable hands. This was fine by me, but Teddy was not a happy camper. He wanted a more dramatic and exciting assignment. Also, he may have been offended by having to work with a mere girl. Fred Fischer asked if we were going to save the nails. He related that during blizzards, he and his sons would sit in the basement and straighten out bent nails. We didn't save these nails, but the statement shows just one more thing that people did to save money during hard times!

When my parents moved from the area, Orville Horning bought out our share of the gravel pit farm. Eventually, he also purchased the Fischer's share. Donald Horning tells me that they sold off the 50 or 60 acres on the west side of the property to the United States Fish and Wildlife Service, and it is now a wildlife sanctuary.

The telephone exchange in Chokio was owned by R W (Curly) Davidson. Farmers were on multiparty lines, and were responsible for maintaining those lines. Everyone on the line had a specific ring that they would answer. For instance, 3 shorts would be someone, 2 longs & a short someone else & so forth. Of course, everyone on the line heard every ring, and often wondered what, who or why someone was calling you. They or you had only to pick up the receiver, listen in and you could answer all those questions, and with any luck get some gossipy news. This was called rubber necking. Even this derogatory term did little to discourage the practice.

The line maintenance was not a fun job. It meant getting calls from fellow line members complaining of the service. Also, the lines were far from being in a top notch state of repair, so problems were frequent, and often occurred at inconvenient or busy times. There was no financial remuneration as the job was considered community service, which anyone should be happy to provide. Right? This is the only community service job I can think of that my father refused to do. Then, one day we came home from town, and all the line maintenance equipment was sitting on our door step. That is how he got the job. I rode around with him sometimes looking for problems. I was to watch for tangled lines mostly. The state of things was so bad, that if a pole was down, someone would have attached the phone line to a fence post. I think my father got rid of this job by moving into Chokio to live.

There was one big advantage however to this phone service. The operator, called central, was a fountain of information. She would be looking out the window right there on Main Street, and knew who was in town, and probably why they were in town. Mother would call her sometimes and say, "Do you know where Duane is?" She usually did, and would dial the appropriate store so Mother could relate her message, like please bring a loaf of bread home. Also, she kept the community informed of births, deaths, etc. She listened in on conversations, too. This could be where Lily Tomlin got her material for Ernestine, the phone operator on Laugh-In. However, no one complained very much, as we all shared in the joys and sorrows of the other residents. We knew each other and cared about each other.

In 1947 we took our first trip other than visiting relatives. My father's younger brother, Verlyn, was a newly wed and we invited him and Marie, his new wife, to accompany us to the Black Hills and Yellowstone National Park. We were still driving the 1938 Buick, which did overheat going across South Dakota. We had to drive a short distance off the highway to a farm and ask for water for the radiator. The farmer said that several people had already stopped that day for water. Otherwise, everything went well, and we all enjoyed it except someone had a cold when we started out, and everyone had it at one time or another before we got home. We did the usual stupid tourist things like feeding the bears in Yellowstone, but no adverse things happened as a result. Yellowstone Park still remains one of my favorite places in the country.

One day, during my senior year, Betty Dierks a classmate, and I were studying in the library when Gladys Laughead came in, and asked us to step out into the hall. When we got out there, she informed us that Betty's father had been killed in an accident. Betty was the oldest child in a family of four children. Robert Dierks, her brother, was a junior, Marilyn, a freshman, and Daryl was in grade school. The family did stay on the farm, and some of them still live in the Chokio area. Betty married, moved to North Dakota and has since died from cancer. Betty is the friend that encouraged me to read. She was an avid reader, and I was not. She kept recommending books to me, and eventually, I developed a love of reading, too. Betty was also our class valedictorian. All that reading had paid off.

From time to time, LaVonne & I would start complaining about how the school was being run. One evening at the supper table, my father said he thought it was run rather well. One of us, I can't remember which, said something like, "What about the students being locked in the gym during lunch hour?" At that time, the gym doubled as a lunch room, and to enter the gym you had to pass through a narrow hallway that went right past the boiler room. All the doors in the gym were locked, hence the only way out was by the boiler room, an obvious disaster in the making in case of a fire. The next day, when we got home from school, my father asked if the gym was locked that day. When we said no, he related that he had paid a call on the superintendent. The man said he just wanted to see how long before anyone would complain. The gym doors remained unlocked after that.

In the spring of 1949, I graduated with my classmates from Chokio High School, and entered nurse's training at Fairview Hospital School of Nursing in Minneapolis that September, but that is another story.

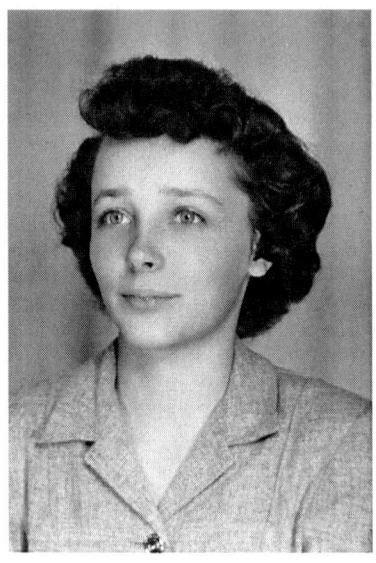

High School graduation

Norma Jipson Knight

2010

Epilogue

Today, Chokio is still a good place to live, but there have been many changes. It has become a retirement community for the most part, which testifies to the loyalty and attachment the locals feel for their community. As the farm sizes increased after WWII, secondary to the advent of ever larger farm implements, the rural population diminished. Many farm building sites were left vacant, and even destroyed to put those acres back into crop production as well. This resulted in fewer children of school age, and eventually the Chokio School combined with the town to the east, Alberta, to form the Chokio-Alberta school system.

The end of gas rationing, together with the end of the 35 mph speed limit and new cars for nearly everyone, enabled people to be more mobile, and they became willing to travel farther to get their groceries, and other needs. Chokio businesses began closing as they could not compete with larger stores, and more complete business centers. Today, there are many fewer businesses than when I resided there. The town does have more houses, but no more population, and perhaps even less. The rural population is much smaller also, as farms have expanded in size.

The United Methodist Church was closed in 2009. Most members now attend services at the Pepperton Methodist Church, which is a rural church north of Alberta. Both congregations had shrunk to such an extent that it was no longer feasible to continue services in both. It was a sad day for those involved, I am sure, when that happened. I feel sad about it even though I no longer live in the area.

There were 23 students in my graduating class, and today fourteen remain alive. Cancer has taken a considerable toll, as you have seen. On the surface, the area appears relatively free of toxic substances, but radon does lurk under ground. This very likely is a contributing factor.

What the future holds for this little community is hard to say, but I have considerable confidence in the people that live there, and their ability to adapt, thrive and live their lives as they wish. God's speed to them all!

Acknowledgements

Thanks are due to several people for the creation of this book. First, to my daughter Kay; thanks for coming up with the suggestion which made the whole project possible when I had no idea that people would be this interested. My husband, Charles, has been most helpful both encouraging and critiquing as well as supplying many suggestions for inclusion. He has heard these stories before. Charles has done much of the work on the photos with Carmen Mami helping out when needed. Carmen also has helped with proof reading. My son, Steven Carlson, also spent a part of his vacation time doing some proof reading.

Friends and relatives have contributed photos, confirmed dates, names, etc as needed. They have also supplied bits of information that I was missing. These include Lillian and Leo Benham, Lowell Carlson, Donald Horning, Verlyn Jipson and Elwood Johnson. Lois and Lennie Stein deserve mention for the incredible encouragement that they gave me and many helpful suggestions. Darlene Nielsen offered both help and encouragement. Her daughter, Shelly Barsuhn, who has authored several books, contributed good advice as well as encouragement.

A special thank you goes to Kay Grossman and the Chokio Review for the right to use the Chokio skyline logo. It was a most generous gesture on their part. The skyline regularly appears at the heading of the weekly editions of the Chokio Review.